Perspectives on Peirce

Perspectives on Peirce

Critical Essays on
Charles Sanders Peirce

edited by Richard J. Bernstein

GREENWOOD PRESS, PUBLISHERS
WESTPORT, CONNECTICUT

Library of Congress Cataloging in Publication Data

Bernstein, Richard J   ed.
    Perspectives on Peirce.

    Reprint of the ed. published by Yale University
Press, New Haven.
    Includes bibliographical references and index.
    1. Peirce, Charles Santiago Sanders, 1839-1914--
Addresses, essays, lectures. I. Title.
[B945.P44B4 1980]   191   80-13703
ISBN 0-313-22414-5 (lib. bdg.)

Originally published with assistance from the foundation
established in memory of James Wesley Cooper of the
Class of 1865, Yale College.

Reprinted with the permission of Yale University Press.

Reprinted in 1980 by Greenwood Press,
a division of Congressional Information Service, Inc.
88 Post Road West, Westport, Connecticut 06881

Printed in the United States of America

10 9 8 7 6 5 4 3 2 1

Preface

Charles Sanders Peirce was a philosopher's philosopher. He was a practicing scientist, an outstanding logician, and a careful student of medieval philosophy and the history of science. He combined enormous erudition, creative scholarship, and a bold speculative imagination. His philosophic temper was both "tough-minded" and "tender-minded." Despite lack of recognition, extreme poverty in his later years, and disease, he tenaciously worked away at his philosophic investigations for more than fifty years.

Anyone who has thought seriously about philosophic issues will find Peirce's writings exciting and provocative. His work is overflowing in insights; one can turn again and again to him for intellectual stimulation. Although Peirce is now being recognized as America's most original—perhaps even its greatest—philosopher, he is still just a name to many. There are a variety of reasons for this lack of knowledge and appreciation. Much of his writing is difficult; at times he was perversely obscure. Although there is ample evidence that he could write lucidly, and even dramatically, he rarely condescended to popularize his ideas. He did not care about explicating his doctrines to those who lacked the intellectual background to understand him, or to those who did not study him seriously, and unfortunately this included most of his contemporaries. Writing in almost total intellectual isolation also marred his work with idiosyncrasies. The greater part of his *Collected Papers* was unpublished during his lifetime. There is still a significant quantity of material not yet published. The philosophic world came to realize the depth, variety, and power of Peirce's philosophy when Charles Hartshorne and Paul

v

Preface

Weiss edited the first six volumes of the *Collected Papers*. They showed a systematic order in what had appeared to be a disarray of papers and fragments.

The following essays testify to the richness and vitality of Peirce's thought. Although the interests of the contributors—all of whom are members of the Yale Philosophy Department—range over the entire field of philosophy, each has been influenced by Peirce in his own thought, and each has previously made a contribution to Peirce scholarship. The essays vary greatly in their treatment of Peirce and the problems raised by him. Rulon Wells has sought to understand in what distinctive ways Peirce is an American. Norwood Russell Hanson's own investigations of 'the logic of discovery' have their roots in Peirce's work. His essay, a lucid reformulation of what is at stake in the idea of a logic of discovery, shows how several approaches to the issue can be traced to suggestions in Peirce. Richard J. Bernstein argues that the concepts of action, conduct, and self-control are tightly and systematically interrelated. Although he finds difficulties in Peirce's theory of the self, he argues that Peirce's insights provide a basis for a fruitful dialogue with contemporary philosophic investigations. John E. Smith, a foremost interpreter of the notion of the community in American philosophy, scrutinizes critically the role of the community in Peirce's philosophy. Finally, Paul Weiss provides a comprehensive overview of Peirce's philosophy indicating Peirce's strengths and weaknesses.

All of the essays are at once sympathetic and sharply critical of what is judged inadequate or false. This is the spirit that Peirce favored and embodied in his work. This book represents the efforts of a "community of inquirers" whose interest in Peirce has been a means for furthering philosophic inquiry itself. Collectively, these essays—based on lectures delivered at Yale University commemorating the fiftieth anniversary of Peirce's death—provide a series of perspectives on Peirce.

In addition to the five essays written especially for this book, we are fortunate in being able to reprint as an introduction the succinct and vivid portrait of Peirce written by Paul Weiss in 1934 for the *Dictionary of American Biography*. Charles Scribner's

Preface

Sons has generously granted permission to reprint this biography in its entirety. It is our hope that the introduction and the essays will help further the critical evaluation and appreciation of Peirce's contribution to philosophy and will encourage the reader to have his own encounter with Peirce's work.

Mr. John Bacon assisted in reading proof, and Mrs. Marge Keller helped in preparing the index. It has been a joy to work with Mrs. Jane Isay of the Yale University Press because of her alertness, patience, sensitivity, and enthusiasm.

References to Peirce's *Collected Papers* follow the standard form of listing the volume and paragraph number, e.g. 5.213. The first six volumes of the *Collected Papers of Charles Sanders Peirce* (Harvard University Press, Cambridge, Mass., 1931–1935) were edited by Charles Hartshorne and Paul Weiss. Volumes 7 and 8 were edited by Arthur W. Burks and were published in 1957 and 1958. The most complete bibliography of Peirce's writings appears in Volume 8. A supplement to this bibliography and a list of writings on Peirce has been prepared for *Studies in the Philosophy of Charles Sanders Peirce, Second Series,* edited by Edward C. Moore and Richard Robin (University of Massachusetts Press, Amherst, 1964). At present, the Peirce manuscripts are being microfilmed by Harvard University and will soon be available to scholars.

R. J. B.

Contents

Introduction   Biography of Charles S. Peirce*

Paul Weiss

PEIRCE, CHARLES SANDERS (Sept. 10, 1839–Apr. 19, 1914), philosopher, logician, scientist, the founder of pragmatism, was born
in Cambridge, Mass., the second son of Benjamin Peirce and
Sarah Hunt (Mills) Peirce, daughter of Elijah Hunt Mills. He
was a brother of James Mills Peirce. His father, the foremost
American mathematician of his time, an inspiring and unconven-
tional teacher, and a man of forceful character and wide interests,
supervised the boy's education to such an extent that Charles
could later say, "he educated me, and if I do anything it will be
his work." However, Charles had learned to read and to write
without the usual course of instruction. He had had independent
recourse to encyclopedias and other works for information on
out-of-the-way subjects. He showed an intense interest in puzzles,
complicated and mathematical card tricks, chess problems, and
code languages, some of which he invented for the amusement
of his playmates. At eight he began to study chemistry of his own
accord, and at twelve set up his own chemical laboratory, experi-
menting with Liebig's bottles of quantitative analysis. At thirteen
he had read and more or less mastered Whately's *Elements of
Logic* (1826). His father trained him in the art of concentration.
From time to time they would play rapid games of double dummy
together, from ten in the evening until sunrise, the father sharply

*This is a reprint of Paul Weiss' biography written in 1934 for the *Dictionary
of American Biography, 14*, 398–403. The editor wishes to express his appreciation to Charles Scribner's Sons for granting permission to reprint the biography
in its entirety.

criticizing every error. In later years this training perhaps helped Charles, though ill and in pain, to write with undiminished power far into the night. His father also encouraged him to develop his power of sensuous discrimination, and later, having put himself under the tutelage of a *sommelier* at his own expense, Charles became a connoisseur of wines. The father's main efforts, however, were directed towards Charles's mathematical education. Rarely was any general principle or theorem disclosed to the son. Instead, the father would present him with problems, tables, or examples, and encouraged him to work out the principles for himself. Charles was also sent to local private schools and then to the Cambridge High School, where he was conspicuous for his declamations. After a term at E. S. Dixwell's school, where he was prepared for college, he entered Harvard in 1855. At college he again had the benefit of his father's instruction. About that time, they also began to have frequent discussions together, in which, pacing up and down the room, they would deal with problems in mathematics beyond even the purview of the elder brother, himself destined to become a mathematician. Charles was graduated from Harvard in 1859, one of the youngest in his class. But his scholastic record was poor. He was seventy-first out of ninety-one for the four years, and in the senior year ranked seventy-ninth. He was apparently too young and of too independent a mind to distinguish himself under the rigid Harvard system of those days.

His father wanted him to be a scientist. Peirce hesitated. Not only was he doubtful whether he should devote himself to a life with so few material benefits, but he was drawn to philosophy as well. At college he had already read Schiller's *Ästhetische Briefe,* and had been led to a study of Kant's *Kritik der reinen Vernunft* which he knew "almost by heart." In July 1861, however, he joined the United States Coast Survey, with which he remained for thirty years, living wherever his investigations led him. About that time he also spent six months studying the technique of classification with Agassiz. In 1862 he received an M.A. degree from Harvard and the next year the degree of Sc.B. in chemistry, *summa cum laude,* the first of its kind. But the interest in philosophy persisted. In 1864–65 he lectured at Harvard on the philosophy of

Biography of Charles Sanders Peirce

science, and as one of a select group which included Ralph Waldo Emerson, George Park Fisher, James Elliott Cabot, and John Fiske he gave the university lectures in philosophy for 1869–70. The next year he was the university lecturer on logic. Meanwhile, from 1869 to 1872, he worked as an assistant at the Harvard Observatory and, from 1872 to 1875, there made the astronomical observations contained in *Photometric Researches* (1878), the only book of his published in his lifetime. It contains material still of value. In 1871 he was in temporary charge of the Coast Survey and the following year became an assistant there, holding the latter position until 1884. In 1873 he was made assistant computer for the nautical almanac and placed in charge of gravity investigations. Two years later, in 1875, he was sent abroad to make pendulum investigations, and to attend, as the first American delegate, the international geodetic conference. His report there that pendulum experiments were subject to a hitherto undetected inaccuracy aroused great discussion and much opposition. But he returned two years later, after the other delegates had had the opportunity to investigate his results, to receive a vote of approval of the congress. Plantamour and Cellerier have acknowledged their indebtedness to him, and his originality in pendulum work has been signalized by Helmert. In that year (1877) he was elected fellow of the American Academy of Arts and Sciences and a member of the National Academy of Science. He had charge of the weights and measures of the United States Coast and Geodetic Survey in 1884–85; was a member of the assay commission of 1888, sat on the international commission of weights and measures, and from 1884 to 1891 was retained as a special assistant in gravity research. But in 1891, either because his experiments had proved too costly or his operations too leisurely, or because of his dissatisfaction with the conduct of the Survey, he ceased to work for the government, and terminated his active scientific career. It was he who first attempted to use the wave length of a light ray as a standard unit of measure, a procedure which has since played an important role in modern metrology. Though inaccuracies have been reported, his scientific work has, for the most part, been lauded by competent men for its precision.

Paul Weiss

Peirce said that he had been brought up in a laboratory, but he always called himself a logician. Originally led to a study of logic by his philosophic problems, he soon saw philosophy and other subjects almost entirely from a logical perspective. In 1847 George Boole, the founder of modern logic, published *The Mathematical Analysis of Logic,* to be followed in 1854 by his definitive work, *An Investigation of the Laws of Thought.* These works, destined to revolutionize the entire science of logic and free it from the thrall of the Aristotelian syllogism, were practically unnoticed in America until Peirce, in 1867, in a short but important paper read before the American Academy of Arts and Sciences (*Proceedings,* Mar. 12, 1867, vol. VII, 250–61; *Collected Papers,* vol. III), referred to Boole's work and made a number of vital and permanent improvements in the Boolean system. He proposed at that time to publish an original logical paper every month, but soon gave up the attempt because insufficient interest was shown in his published work. Nevertheless, for almost fifty years, from 1866 until the end of his life, while with the Survey and after he left it, he occupied himself with logic in all its branches. His technical papers of 1867 to 1885 established him as the greatest formal logician of his time, and the most important single force in the period from Boole to Ernst Schröder. These papers are difficult, inaccessible, scattered, and fragmentary, and their value might never have been known if it had not been that Schröder based a large portion of his *Vorlesungen über die Algebra der Logik* (3 vols., in 4, 1890–1905) on them, and called attention to the high character of Peirce's contributions. He radically modified, extended, and transformed the Boolean algebra, making it applicable to propositions, relations, probability, and arithmetic. Practically single-handed, following De Morgan, Peirce laid the foundations of the logic of relations, the instrument for the logical analysis of mathematics. He invented the copula of inclusion, the most important symbol in the logic of classes, two new logical algebras, two new systems of logical graphs, discovered the link between the logic of classes and the logic of propositions, was the first to give the fundamental principle for the logical development of mathematics, and made exceedingly important contributions

4

Biography of Charles Sanders Peirce

to probability theory, induction, and the logic of scientific methodology. He completed an elaborate work on logic but could not get it published. It was too specialized for the publishers, who preferred elementary textbooks and perhaps the writings of a man in an academic chair. Many of his more important writings on logic, among which are his detailed papers on his new science of semiotics, he never published, and the final appreciation of his full strength and importance as a logician awaits the assimilation of the posthumous papers.

Benjamin Peirce, in a public address in the late sixties, said that he expected Charles to go beyond him in mathematics. In the early eighties, J. J. Sylvester, the great mathematician of the day, is reported to have said of Charles that he was "a far greater mathematician than his father." However, Charles published only a few papers on pure mathematics. His concern was with the more difficult and fascinating problem of its foundations. In 1867 in his paper, "Upon the Logic of Mathematics" (*Proceedings of the American Academy of Arts and Sciences,* Sept. 10, 1867, vol. VII, 402–12; *Collected Papers,* vol. III), he clearly anticipated the method for the derivation and definition of number employed in the epochal *Principia Mathematica* (3 vols., 1910–13) of A. N. Whitehead and Bertrand Russell. He edited with important notes and addenda (*Collected Papers,* vol. III) his father's *Linear Associative Algebra* (in *American Journal of Mathematics,* July, Sept. 1881), having originally, in the sixties, interested his father in that work. He showed, among other things, that every associative algebra can be represented by one whose elements are matrices. He also made a number of contributions, over a period of years, to the theory of aggregates and transfinite arithmetic, his work often anticipating or running parallel with the heralded work of Richard Dedekind and Georg Cantor. Many of his unpublished studies in such subjects as analysis situs were subsequently repeated by other and independent investigators. Had all his mathematical papers been published in his lifetime, he would have been a more important factor in the history of mathematics than he is today. His work on the logical and philosophical problems of mathematics remains, however, among the foremost in the field.

Pragmatism, Peirce's creation, had its origin in the discussions, in Cambridge, of a fortnightly "metaphysical club" founded in the seventies. Oliver Wendell Holmes, the jurist, John Fiske, and Francis E. Abbot were members. But more important for the history of pragmatism were Chauncey Wright, a philosopher of power with whom Peirce had frequent heated but profitable discussions; William James, Peirce's lifelong friend and benefactor, in whose honor he seems later to have adopted the middle name "Santiago" ("St. James" in Spanish); and Nicholas St. John Green, a lawyer and follower of Bentham who had a tendency to interpret doctrines in terms of their effect upon social life. It had been Kant's emphasis on formal logic which drove Peirce to take up that subject, the history of which he studied with characteristic thoroughness. His interest in the history of logic, in turn, was largely responsible for his contact with the schoolmen. By 1871 he was converted to Duns Scotus' version of realism, a position which he held throughout his life. In the very paper in which Peirce first expounded his Scotistic realism and criticized the nominalism of Berkeley, he roughly outlined the pragmatic position (*North American Review,* Oct. 1871, pp. 449–72). The first definite statement of Peirce's on the pragmatic principle, as it is alternatively called, was not given, however, until 1878. It is contained in a paper, originally written in French in 1877 while he was on his way to the international geodetic conference, later translated by him into English, and published in the *Popular Science Monthly* in January 1878, under the title "How to Make Our Ideas Clear." It was the second of a series of six articles dealing mainly with problems in logic (Nov. 1877, Jan., Mar., Apr., June, Aug. 1878; *Collected Papers,* vol. V, book II; vol. II, book III, B; vol. VI, book I). Together with the first paper of that series which he translated into French, it was published in the *Revue Philosophique* (Dec. 1878, Jan. 1879). In that article he formulated, as the most important device for making ideas clear, the principle that we are to "Consider what effects, which might conceivably have practical bearings, we conceive the object of our conception to have. Then, our conception of these effects is the whole of our conception of the object" (*Popular Science*

Biography of Charles Sanders Peirce

Monthly, Jan. 1878, p. 293; *Collected Papers,* vol. V, par. 402). This formula has been ridiculed for its awkward and somewhat bewildering repetition, but Peirce contended that he chose each word deliberately, wishing to emphasize that it was concerned with concepts and not with things and was a principle of method rather than a proposition in metaphysics. As usual, he was to receive no recognition for his work until another man called attention to it much later. In 1898 William James first publicly used the term "pragmatism" and acknowledged Peirce's priority in the creation of the doctrine and the name it bears. Peirce's pragmatism, however, is not the same as James's; it has more in common with the somewhat independently developed idealism of Josiah Royce and the later views of John Dewey. In fact, when James heard Peirce lecture on pragmatism in 1903 he confessed that he could not understand him. On the other hand, Peirce soon rebelled against the characteristic twists which James and others gave to pragmatism. In 1905 he coined the term "pragmaticism," which was "ugly enough to be safe from kidnappers" (*Monist,* Apr. 1905, p. 166; *Collected Papers,* V, par. 414), to characterize his own views; these included much (such as the idea of an Absolute and a belief in universals) that the other pragmatists were disposed to discard. For his version of the doctrine he had but few supporters, and most of these were not in America.

Peirce did share, though, many of the views characteristic of the pragmatic school, developing them in his own, independent fashion. He was a firm believer in the dependence of logic on ethics, argued as early as 1868 against individualism and egoism, and developed social theories of reality and logic. His most important published philosophical contributions, however, are those that embody his cosmology. They are contained in a series of five articles written for the *Monist* (Jan. 1891–Jan. 1893; *Collected Papers,* vol. VI). There he vigorously opposed the mechanical philosophy, defended the reality of absolute chance and the principle of continuity, attempting to solve the hallowed problem of the relation of mind and body, to explain the origin of law, to account for the impossibility of exactly verifying the laws of nature, and to develop his theory of an evolutionary universe.

Dewey, James, and Paul Carus, among others, were quick to recognize their importance. The latter, who was the editor of the *Monist,* engaged Peirce in controversy, providing him with some of the space necessary for the further clarification of his position. Though Peirce's tychism, or theory of absolute chance, received more consideration and favorable attention, it was his synechism, or doctrine of continuity, which he considered his real contribution to philosophy, holding it to be, however, a regulative principle rather than an ultimate absolute metaphysical doctrine. His characteristic metaphysical views do not seem to have been wholeheartedly accepted by any established philosopher during his lifetime, though James, Royce, and Dewey have unmistakably acknowledged his influence.

Peirce was not given the opportunity to teach for more than eight years during his entire life. His longest academic connection was with the Johns Hopkins University where he was a lecturer on logic from 1879 to 1884. Apart from his early Harvard University lectures of 1864, 1869, and 1870, he lectured three times before the Lowell Institute: in 1866 on logic, in 1892 on the history of science, and in 1903 on logic. The only other official or semi-official contact he seems to have had with students was through a lecture on number at Bryn Mawr in 1896, three or four lectures on "detached topics" delivered at Mrs. Ole Bull's in Cambridge in 1898, his seven lectures on pragmatism at Harvard before the philosophy club at Harvard in 1907. Yet he was an inspiring teacher. Too advanced perhaps for the ordinary student, he was a vital formative factor in the lives of the more progressive ones, who remembered him later with affection and reverence. He treated them as intellectual equals and impressed them as having a profound knowledge of his subject. Of his small class in logic at Johns Hopkins, four, one of whom was Christine Ladd-Franklin, made lasting contributions to the subject in a book which he edited and to which he contributed (*Studies in Logic. By Members of the Johns Hopkins University,* 1883). His love of precision made it impossible for him to make a popular appeal, and he had no capacity for making himself clear to large numbers. This failing would perhaps have been considerably overcome if he had had the opportunity to come into more contact with students who challenged his statements and demanded explications. There is some justice in James's remark that Peirce's lectures were "flashes of brilliant light relieved against Cimmerian darkness" (*Pragmatism*, 1907, p. 5), though the lectures on pragmatism, which this phrase was supposed to characterize, are lucid when placed against the background of his entire system. He would buttress his ideas with a technical vocabulary, creating odd new terms in his attempt to articulate new ideas, trying to cover vast fields in limited space. He did at times show a sudden gift for clear expression, but he lacked the ability to know where further explanation was necessary.

He was eager to teach, but personal difficulties barred his way. He had described himself when a senior at college as being vain, snobbish, uncivil, reckless, lazy, and ill-tempered. He certainly was not lazy out of college. But he was always somewhat proud of his ancestry and connections, overbearing towards those who stood in his way, indifferent to the consequences of his acts, quick to take affront, highly emotional, easily duped, and with, as he puts it, "a reputation for not finding things." He was irregular in his hours, forgetful of his personal appearance. This dark-bearded man of stocky build and medium height with a short neck and bright dark eyes could, however, be charming at social gatherings, recite with skill and converse delightfully; he was singularly free from academic jealousy, and he could work twenty hours at a stretch on a subject for which he had for years failed to find a publisher. A "queer being" James called him. Peirce himself felt there was something peculiar in his inheritance and put emphasis on the fact that he was left-handed. He could, however, write with both hands—in fact, he was capable of writing a question with one hand and the answer simultaneously with the other. In his years of early promise his peculiar traits were certainly no serious handicap to an academic career. But not only, as he regretted, had his father neglected to teach him moral self-control, so that he later "suffered unspeakably," but he had domestic difficulties as well. On Oct. 16, 1862, when twenty-three years old, he had married Harriet Melusina Fay, three years his senior, a granddaughter of Bishop John Henry Hopkins. She joined him in his early scientific work, was respected in Cambridge circles, and afterward distinguished herself as an organizer and writer. He divorced her on Apr. 24, 1883, in Baltimore, alleging she had deserted him in October 1876. Shortly afterward, he writes that he married Juliette Froissy of Nancy, France, with whom he lived for the rest of his life and who survived him. His difficulties with his first wife seem to have been an important factor in his loss of academic standing and the partial estrangement of his friends and relatives.

Having inherited some money, he retired in 1887, when only forty-eight years old, to "the wildest county of the Northern States" near Milford, Pa. There he secured a house and tract of land, and fortressed by his large and select library of scientific and philosophic works, many of which were of considerable value, he devoted himself to his writings on logic and philosophy. At the same time he wrote all the definitions on logic, metaphysics, mathematics, mechanics, astronomy, astrology, weights, measures, and universities for the *Century Dictionary* (6 vols., 1889–91), and a gradually increasing number of book reviews on a wide range of topics for the *Nation*. He records that he wrote about 2,000 words a day. This was done with care and in a clear hand. Having a remarkable capacity for self-criticism, on which he prided himself, he would work over his copy, rewriting it as often as a dozen times, until it was as accurate and as precisely worded as he could make it. More often than not, the final manuscript, which might have involved weeks of work, would not be published, but together with all the preceding drafts and miscellaneous scraps incidental to its writing would be allowed to remain on his tables. Immediately, with the same enthusiasm, he would begin another formulation or start on a new topic, to be subjected to the same treatment. He has characterized himself as having the persistency of a wasp in a bottle.

As a young man he had little control over his money; he always remained extravagant. By his retirement from the Survey, he had cut off his government salary of $3,000, and had to live on what he could glean from his occasional lectures, sales of his books, translations, private tutoring, collaboration on dictionaries, work

Biography of Charles Sanders Peirce

as a consultant, and from private donations. In his home he built an attic where he could work undisturbed or, by pulling up the ladder, escape from his creditors. Though he had been employed by J. M. Baldwin in 1901 to write most of the articles on logic for the *Dictionary of Philosophy and Psychology* (3 vols. in 4, 1901–05), by 1902 he was in debt and on the verge of poverty, doing his own chores and dissipating his energies in small tasks in order to obtain immediate funds. He then applied to the Carnegie Fund for aid in getting his works published. Nine years before he had planned a twelve-volume work on philosophy, which he had to give up, despite many indorsements from leading persons, for lack of subscribers. Now he proposed to submit thirty-six memoirs, "each complete in itself, forming a unitary system of logic in all its parts." These memoirs were to be submitted one at a time and to be paid for when and as approved. Though his proposed memoirs would have dealt with vital issues, and though his application was accompanied by eulogistic letters from the greatest men of the time, his application was rejected, the official reason being that logic was outside the scope of the fund, not being a "natural science." By 1906 he had ceased to review for the *Nation* and had lost most of his other sources of income; the next year he was practically penniless. Under James a small fund, barely enough to keep Peirce and his wife alive, was secured for him through appeals to old friends and appreciative students. He published for three years—papers on logic, pragmatism, epistemology, and religion which are among the best he ever wrote. By 1909 he was a very ill man of seventy, compelled to take a grain of morphine daily to stave off the pain. With undiminished persistency, forming his letters to judge from the tremulous, painstaking script with great difficulty, he kept on writing—or rather rewriting, for by that time he had finally ceased to be original. Five years later he died of cancer, a frustrated, isolated man, still working on his logic, without a publisher, with scarcely a disciple, unknown to the public at large.

After his death his manuscripts were bought from his wife by the Harvard philosophy department (for their publication, see bibliography). There are hundreds of them, without dates, with

11

leaves missing, unpaginated and disordered; there are duplicates and fragments, repetitions and restatements. His interests were not restricted to logic, pragmatism, metaphysics, mathematics, geodesy, religion, astronomy, and chemistry. He also wrote on psychology, early English and classical Greek pronunciation, psychical research, criminology, the history of science, ancient history, Egyptology, and Napoleon, prepared a thesaurus and an editor's manual, and did translations from Latin and German. James called Peirce the most original thinker of their generation; Peirce placed himself somewhere near the rank of Leibniz. This much is now certain; he is the most original and versatile of America's philosophers and America's greatest logician.

[For years futile attempts were made to organize Peirce's papers; he had himself said that he could not have put them together. In 1927, however, Charles Hartshorne and Paul Weiss thought they saw a systematic connection between most of them, and prepared a ten-volume selection, now in process of publication as *Collected Papers of Charles Sanders Peirce* (5 vols., 1931–34).[1] The foregoing sketch is based mainly on these papers, autobiographical notes, and letters and reminiscences of his relatives, friends, and pupils. See also R. S. Rantoul, *Essex Institute Hist. Colls.*, XVIII (1881), 161–76; articles in *Jour. of Philosophy, Psychology and Scientific Methods,* Dec. 21, 1916, by Josiah Royce, Fergus Kernan, John Dewey, Christine Ladd-Franklin, Joseph Jastrow, and M. R. Cohen; *Chance, Love and Logic* (1923), ed. by M. R. Cohen, containing some of Peirce's published philosophical papers, an introduction, and an almost complete bibliography; F. C. Russell, "In Memoriam Charles S. Peirce," *Monist* (July 1914); E. W. Davis, "Charles Peirce at Johns Hopkins," *Mid-West Quart.* (Oct. 1914); *Harvard College, Records of the Class of 1859* (1896); F. C. Peirce, *Peirce Genealogy* (1880); obituary in *Boston Evening Transcript,* Apr. 21, 1914.]

1. Ten volumes were projected, of which 6 were completed under the editorship of Weiss and Hartshorne. Volumes 7 and 8, the final volumes published by Harvard, have been edited by Arthur W. Burks. R. J. B.

Chapter 1   Charles S. Peirce as an American

Rulon Wells

PEIRCE AS A CRITIC OF AMERICA

Charles Peirce lived for the first thirty years of his life in Cambridge, Massachusetts, and for the last thirty in Milford, Pennsylvania. He was therefore in some sense an American. But it is not easy to find ways in which he was *in any notable way or degree* an American. He was proud of his Yankee, Boston, and Harvard background, but he was not, in the eyes of most contemporaries, a worthy scion of it. Lacking adequate self-control in his social relations,[1] he alienated enough people to spoil his career and his life.

But the alienation has a significant pattern and a deeper meaning. One of the reasons (not the only reason) why he alienated people was that he was critical, and outspoken in his criticism. By natural inclination he cast himself in the role of critic. Not that he was a critic only; his positive, creative powers were enormous. But criticism always played its part; criticism—reaction, a variety of Secondness—was always the first step. He was a logician,[2] and (4.9; 5.108) logic is the critic (i.e. the critique) of arguments.

The critical attitude looms large in Peirce. We can generalize and say that it is one aspect of a spirit of opposition that governs

1. See Introduction above, p. 9; Murray G. Murphey, *The Development of Peirce's Philosophy* (Cambridge, Mass., 1961), pp. 17–19.
2. See 2.662–63 and 2.760 (he began the study of logic in 1852); 3.322 (contrasts himself, a logician, with Sylvester, a mathematician); 4.239 (himself a logician, his father a mathematician).

him, to the point of tyranny. He was brought up, he tells us,[3] in a Unitarian household. What was his reaction to this? He joined the Episcopal Church. He claimed that his act was intended to unify; but it certainly didn't unify him with his family. Did it, then, unify him with his fellow Episcopalians? "I say the creed in church along with the rest," he explains, "but without believing anything but the general essence and spirit of it."

Another instance of his instinctive, spontaneous opposition is worth mentioning. His friend and benefactor Paul Carus proposed to write on the marriage of science and religion. Peirce found the proposal amusing (6.603), because the conciliation of science and religion would be a 'birth of time' without the good doctor's help. Yet in that same year Peirce published in Carus' journal a paper (6.428–34) making exactly the same proposal, with the explanation that though the 'marriage' (or, as he calls it in 7.578, the 'onement') would take place sooner or later without help, help would hasten it.

The critical orientation entails for Peirce a twofold relation to America which, misunderstood, would look like simple ambivalence. Distinguishing himself from America—setting himself over against America, as the idealists would say—he functions as critic; identifying himself with America, he functions as American.

What Peirce has to say as a critic of America[4] is not original, but it is thoroughly consistent with his general philosophy, which *is* original. His forthright declaration to Lady Victoria Welby (Lieb, p. 28) that "the people ought to be enslaved" could be taken as undemocratic in sentiment; but when his exasperation has finished exploding, he announces a plan—time prevents him from divulging it to his correspondent—for educating the people to improve themselves. His general principles dictate that the goals of knowledge and love be reached as soon as possible, but

3. See Murphey, p. 15.

4. Many of his most revealing published remarks are in *Charles S. Peirce's Letters to Lady Welby*, ed. Irwin C. Lieb (New Haven, 1953). Americans are great conservatives; in this country one is expected to be just like everybody else, and to live with everybody else; Americans are afraid to be alone (Lieb, pp. 6, 7, 15). America is a well-regulated country (2.195).

14

the particular question 'What political institutions best serve these goals?' is the matter for a correspondingly particular inquiry.

I have pointed out several instances in which Peirce's criticism has a personal 'edge' to it. That personal quality is no more than an edge, however. Let me add another instance to help show this. Peirce (5.583) trenchantly criticizes Harvard,[5] his alma mater, for its emphasis on gentility and prosperity at the expense of intellectual ruggedness; he finds his private pupils in New York much more receptive to his ideas, and thereupon (1.668) appoints himself an honorary New Yorker. (When Peirce visited New York, he was at pains to inform people that he was from Cambridge and Harvard.) But inasmuch as his basic method of thinking is to think things *through,* without regard to personal comfort or predilection, the criticisms of superficiality and of self-indulgence are the most serious criticisms he can level. And thus, whatever personal animus he may have had in such criticisms, and however well- or ill-founded they may be in individual cases, the charges involved are, in the light of his philosophy, as impersonal and as reasonable as a charge can be.

When Peirce is acting as a critic of America and of things American, his attitude reminds one of Nietzsche's, Nietzsche who said that "To attack is with me a proof of good will."[6] Nietzsche's admirers should remember this in evaluating his own national attitudes. In the light of this clue—"As many as I love, I rebuke and chasten,"[7]—it is plain that Nietzsche held the Germans dear, and regarded the rest of the world as beneath reproof. No one was actually good, but only the Germans had the potentiality; and by this test, Nietzsche was very much of a German nationalist. Whereas Peirce was very little of an American nationalist, and very much a citizen of the world, because he did not confine his well-intentioned critiques to any one country. He was constantly, by this oblique method, demonstrating his regard for his boyhood

5. See Ralph B. Perry, *The Thought and Character of William James* (2 vols. Boston, 1935), 2, 419.

6. *Ecce Homo,* 1.7; Eng. trans., Walter Kaufmann, *Nietzsche* (New York, Meridian Books, 1956), p. 115.

7. Rev. 3:19; cf. Deut. 8:5, Ps. 94:12, Job 5:17, Prov. 3:12, Heb. 12:6.

friend William James; but immediately on striking up a corre-
spondence with Lady Welby he began to offer her similar proofs
of good will.

THE AMERICAN AS UNIFIER

From Peirce as a critic of America, I turn now to Peirce as an
American critic. As I will show on pages 30 ff., Peirce defends
Christian faith, and, as part of his program of unification, is concerned to show that there is a Christian logic. Indeed, he finds
support for the Pragmatic Maxim in the scripture, "By their fruits
ye shall know them." Now his method of synthesizing the thought
of his predecessors, and, especially, of 'welding' the British to
the German outlook, beautifully illustrates the Pauline text (cf.
p. 32, below): "Prove all things; hold fast that which is good."

Before turning attention to Peirce's 'provings', I would like
to review some ways in which an American might be expected to
behave, according to various clichés about America, stereotypes
(1.134; 6.292) proposed by Americans about themselves or by
Europeans about them. Some of these may seem to speak the
truth about Charles Peirce.

The first cliché is that America is a brave new world, a place
capable of a fresh beginning. This may be taken to mean that the
dead hand of the past slackens or wholly relaxes its grip. Peirce
would not readily admit a complete relaxation, because that would
be a discontinuity, but his account of process does provide for
the breakup of old habits, though it says little about the conditions for breakup.

The conception of America as the place of fresh start passes,
by graded transition, into the conception of it as the land of freedom; with regard to ideas this would mean free thought, and,
among other things, freedom (1) to try thinking afresh, (2) to accept or reject ideas that are submitted to it. The first kind of
freedom Peirce scorns; his criticism of Descartes, the great propo-
nent of this freedom, is radical. The second kind he welcomes, and
employs as part of his main method of synthesizing British with
German thought.

Peirce as an American

The ideas of freshness and freedom resemble another feature often thought characteristically American, the trait of looking to the future. America is supposed to be dynamic (compared with the relatively static Old World), energetic, receptive to change and eager for it, and confident that what one doesn't like can be changed. It is with such supposed traits in mind that pragmatism is supposed to be a distinctively and preeminently American philosophy.[8]

I shall put the topic of pragmatism aside in order to concentrate on another feature of America, the fact of unification. It is Peirce's great hope that, just as the several states united themselves into a nation, the entire world will be united through knowledge and through love into a single community. He generalizes unification into a universal norm; though he never puts his point in precisely this way, *e pluribus unum* would perfectly serve as a descriptive phrase for his fundamental process of evolution. If political unification—achieving unity and preserving it—is the most notable social achievement of the American people, then a philosophy that takes unification (in every aspect and every application) as its central phenomenon has a plausible claim to be regarded as the, or a, distinctively American philosophy. This claim which I make on Peirce's behalf is not damaged by his having almost nothing to say about political philosophy as such, for his doctrines are more general, and political philosophy takes its place as a special case. And Peirce interestingly makes the observation (7.264) that nearly all of America's outstanding men were involved either in the War of Independence or in the War Between the States.

For Peirce the great ideal is unification, the achieving of unity; but it cannot be said too soon that unity does not mean uniformity. On the contrary, one of his alternative names for the growth that

8. Neither James nor Peirce made any such claim for it. James in particular made repeated efforts to credit his 'old way of thinking' to Mill, Bain, Shadworth Hodgson, and, with more reserve, F. C. S. Schiller. Peirce (5.34) enjoins himself and likeminded people "not to be influenced by any liking for pragmatism or any pride in it as an American doctrine." In even calling it an American doctrine, Peirce need not be taken to mean more than that it happens to have been proposed by Americans.

leads to unification is *variescence* (Lieb, p. 44). And he shows an awareness that, in its social versions, unity *in* variety is not easy to achieve; for he remarks (see n. 4 above) to his correspondent Lady Welby that "in America everyone is expected to be like everyone else."

To return now to the subject of Peirce as an American critic. Although Peirce was no nationalist it was his lot to play a national role. He was typical of many Americans—perhaps the majority of thoughtful ones—in being sympathetic and responsive to British ideas and ideals. He was typical of many Americans in being sympathetic and responsive to German ideas and ideals. What was atypical and unique in him was his feeling both these sympathies.[9] A person having both affinities is preeminently qualified to feel the need for synthesis. That Charles Peirce was also preeminently qualified to execute the task is another matter.

The first step in unification would be critical selection. Now a genuine unification would not be eclectic, because selection would

---

9. And in feeling them in areas where they obviously conflicted. Many people would sympathize with German literary ideals, but with British political ideals.

In Peirce's personal circle the predominant sympathies were British. Chauncey Wright, especially, declared his British affinities (see Philip P. Wiener, *Evolution and the Founders of Pragmatism* [Cambridge, Mass., 1949], p. 34), and (Wiener, pp. 35, 58–59) analyzed the German inability to 'place' Darwin and his contribution in terms of differences between British and German outlooks. Peirce was conscious (5.12) of the fact that except for himself everybody in the group that he called the Metaphysical Club was British-oriented.

Peirce had, since his teens, been interested in Kant. Other German thinkers also had interested him. He had read Friedrich Schiller's *Ästhetische Briefe* about 1855 with his friend Horatio Paine (2.197; 5.402 n. 3; Lieb, p. 27). Not long afterwards he threw himself into the study of the *Critique of Pure Reason*. This book remained a lifelong influence (Murphey, passim).

Among other criticisms of the Germans, Peirce criticizes their subjectivism (2.165; Lieb, p. 4), their willingness to give thought free rein, their lack of intellectual self-control (8.240), and their consequent tendency to run in packs (1.77; 3.425). Most frequently of all, he attacks their 'higher criticism' (e.g. 7.177).

Besides direct influence from Germany, Peirce felt an indirect influence through the American transcendentalists. He confesses (6.102) that he may have succumbed to transcendentalism, which in 2.113 he classifies with Kantianism.

be only the *first* stage of it. But let us see what would be selected, according to Peirce.

And first, what would be selected *from?* It is clear that our recent heritage comes chiefly from two peoples, the British and the Germans. One may wonder at the omission of the French. Peirce has nothing like the admiration that William James has for recent French philosophers such as Taine, Renouvier, Bergson. One obvious reason is that the recent French contributed little to logic, Peirce's special interest; their doctrines were either bizarre, like the Abbé Gratry's, or essentially unoriginal, like Poincaré's (5.597).

Putting together things that Peirce says—and things he doesn't say—about the various nations, we discover that he regards Descartes as the last major French philosopher. Why the French should be so sterile in philosophy when, without a break from Descartes and Fermat through Laplace at least, they are so eminent in mathematics and natural science (he also cites recent French scholarship with respect) is a puzzle about which Peirce, as far as I can detect, has no conjecture to offer. It may be that French philosophers made original contributions, but that they all partook either of the British mode or of the German, so that though original they were not nationally distinctive. Or, their original contributions may have been completely absorbed, between Peirce's time and their own, by British and German thinkers. Whatever the reason, Peirce feels (1.3–5) that he has to reckon with two main schools of modern philosophy, opposed in their tendencies; if these two schools can be characterized in national terms, say as British and German, that fact is secondary.

The puzzle about the French is heightened by the partiality that Peirce shows for certain aspects (nonphilosophical) of French culture; he lets us know (8.169) that he esteems French etiquette, though not French morals. Ideologically the French influence on nascent America was considerable, not only through particular thinkers like Montesquieu, Voltaire, Rousseau, and the Encyclopedists, but through the political support that France gave to the Colonies in revolt. Peirce apparently gave little thought to this influence; I believe this was mere accidental neglect, mere human limitation, and that taking it into account would enrich his meta-physics—his categories—on the material side. The neglect was accidental: as a matter of genius and temperament Peirce paid little attention to social and political philosophy; as a matter of environmental circumstances Peirce was conscious in his own formative years of just the two national influences I have men-tioned, British and German (cf. n. 9 above).

Peirce's method of synthesis is critical. He singles out some tendency, some attitude, some doctrine, and subjects it to criticism.

Peirce thinks the Germans are too subjective. They are inclined to herd behavior; someone, e.g. Hegel, is in fashion, and it is dangerous to oppose him; then he goes out of fashion, and it is dangerous to support him. Their tendency in logic is psychologis-tic; their way of reducing the *ought* to the *is* is inept. A corrective is to be found in British thought.

The British, for their part, are too sensationalistic. They regard the work of thought as purely an elaboration of sense-data. The Germans' critique of the sense-datum theory points up the in-adequacies of the British theory.

Here, then, are two faults, a German fault corrected by the British and a British fault corrected by the Germans. Let me now cite two virtues—two positive, admirable traits. Peirce admired in Germany that "spirit of getting to the bottom of things" on which Kant (*Critique of Pure Reason,* B xlii) had complimented his fellow countrymen. (Peirce admired the medieval scholastics for the same quality, 1.33–34.) And he admired the British admiration for simplicity, thinking only that they exaggerated their success in conforming to their ideal.[10]

The method that Peirce uses for welding British with German thought is primarily critical. Ideally and in principle the method calls for an inventory of British and of German traits, arranged correspondingly, so that one would then simply run down the inventory and criticize each principle in turn. Peirce does not

10. In his review (8.7–38) of Berkeley's works, Peirce discusses the English penchant for a certain kind of simplicity, and shows how nominalism illustrates this penchant. In 6.7 he objects to the excessive simplicity of English "one-idea'd philosophies."

polish his execution of the method to this degree, but from the samples of the method he gives it is clear that his criticism goes beyond sheer selection. It differs, therefore, from the 'eclectic' method defined by Clement of Alexandria (*Stromateis* 1.37), of simply picking out (*eklegein*) from each way of thought those traits that are best. Nor could Peirce be called simply an arbitrator, because he does not confine himself to adjudicating claims, but may initiate claims of his own. The most famous instance is that he rejects a trait common to British and to German thought, namely what he calls nominalism.

Several previous writers on Peirce have seen his twofold sympathy as an ambivalence; as the very opposite of eclecticism, in which instead of choosing one of two, he inconsistently tries to choose both. Where he tries to keep both viewpoints but gives up in the end, often the German viewpoint is the one he chooses.

A case in point is his view about unity.

The German demand for unity is of the kind that Kant and subsequent philosophers called architectonic. A set of concepts has an architectonic unity if, though there is more than one concept in the set, all the concepts are generated, or placed in relation to one another, by a single principle. Peirce took the architectonic requirement seriously and (6.612) stressed his fidelity to it. British philosophy places little emphasis on unity, on rigor (Husserl's ideal of a *strenge Wissenschaft* is more German than British), or on consistency. Its economy is an economy of means, of getting a job done with a minimum of new or special equipment, an economy that could be characterized as resourcefulness and self-sufficiency eked out by improvisation. This is what Peirce had in mind when (cf. n. 10 above) he charged the British with being 'one-idea'd philosophers.'

TWO AVENUES TO UNITY: KNOWLEDGE AND FAITH

There is a metaphysical doctrine called absolute idealism, of which Peirce's philosophy is a species. The idealistic component will be left out of consideration here. The absolutism, on the other hand, will be of central concern.

21

Peirce holds that, in some way, all the processes in the world are related so intimately that we may properly speak of a single fundamental and universal world process. It is a feature of his absolute idealism to be evolutionary. 'Evolution' is to be understood in a sense generalized[11] beyond the temporal, so that temporal evolution—evolution in time—is only a special case of it. The generalized sense is pseudo-temporal: somehow our understanding of it is grounded in an understanding of time and of genuinely, simply temporal evolution. Pseudo-temporal evolution and becoming may be called, for convenience, pseudo-evolution and pseudo-becoming, and so on.

We need also to acknowledge the doctrine that the pseudo-process has a pseudo-terminus (pseudo-end). This doctrine of Peirce's involves absurdities, as I argue elsewhere,[12] but I will take it for granted here without going into these. The pseudo-terminus of the world is a community of minds; recalling that the best translation of the Greek word *polis* into present-day English is not 'city', 'state', or 'city-state', but 'community', we may compare Peirce's ideal of a world community with the ancient ideal of a *cosmopolis*.

But all of the words 'city', 'state', and 'community' primarily suggest to us a *political* community; and distinctively political concepts (e.g. compromise, coalition, balance of power) are conspicuous in Peirce by their absence. One would be disposed to think that the lack is personal and accidental, the mere effect of Peirce's temperamental predilections, and this reading could find support in Peirce's self-confession. I am, he says (6.184), "a very snarl of twine"; or, as he elsewhere (cf. n. 2 above) says, a logi-

11. Generalizing is the fundamental way in which thought advances, but Peirce now and then (3.454; 4.5) serves notice that he is using the word 'generalize' itself in a generalized sense. He repeatedly (e.g. 2.110) urges that methods of science be generalized, e.g. (6.460; 7.66, 7.81) by adapting a method of one science to another science. See also the end of the Appendix on welding (pp. 40–41 below).

12. See "The True Nature of Peirce's Evolutionism," *Studies in the Philosophy of Charles Sanders Peirce*, ed. Edward C. Moore and Richard Robin, pp. 304–22.

cian. But there is more to it than that; once again, a personal, seemingly accidental fact about Peirce has a deeper significance.

There is room in Peirce's system to develop a political philosophy, but considerable preliminary developments would be necessary to build up to it. Philosophy of religion, by contrast, is much nearer to development; though present (in Peirce's published works) only in outline, and in obiter dicta, the developments needed are not preliminary *to* it, but developments *of* it.

The developments preliminary to a political philosophy would involve such concepts as 'coalition' and 'power bloc'. Many political philosophies work with a set of levels; they set up a political level intermediate between a social level and a level of the church or religious community. The absence of such a level in Peirce is a sign that he believes the levels he does set up—the level of scientific communities and the level of religious communities— are together a sufficient means for the pseudo-evolution of the human race into complete unification.

One of Peirce's favorite names for his main pseudo-evolutionary process is *welding*. (See Appendix, pp. 38 ff. below.) How apt this metaphor is for expressing an absolutist view is shown clearly by contrasting Peirce's use of it with William James'. When James speaks of the absolute idealist as welding things together into an iron block, he speaks with horror. His own picture[13] of a 'pluralistic universe' is developed in explicit opposition to the 'block universe' of Hegel. Peirce believes he has his own way of introducing that freedom in the universe which proved, in the end, to be lacking in Hegel; this is his 'tychism'. With the help of tychism Peirce feels entitled to a 'great hope' that the pseudo-terminus of pseudo-evolution will be a community, society, or colony of minds welded into a continuous whole; the former indi-

13. In "The Dilemma of Determinism" (1884; reprinted in *The Will to Believe* [New York, 1896], p. 150), James speaks of the view that "the whole is in each and every part and welds it with the rest into an absolute unity, an iron block." In 1882 (reprinted in *The Will to Believe,* p. 292) he had written of "the universe of Hegel—the absolute block whose parts have no loose play." The phrase "block universe" is also found in *A Pluralistic Universe* (New York, 1909), pp. 76, 310, 328.

viduals would sacrifice their individuality wherever, and insofar as, preserving it would separate one individual from another.

Now Peirce recognizes two avenues, or routes, to this pseudo-end: the route of science, or knowledge, and the route of religion, or faith. It is essential to his system, not accidental, that no other routes coordinate with these are recognized—not, for example, a route of morality or a route of political action. This is how it is that he envisions a 'marriage' of science and religion; he must, as a monist and absolutist, unify the two unifiers.

Sometimes Peirce treats ethics as strictly dependent on religion, sometimes as independent of it. The reason for the double treatment is that sometimes he deals with conduct aimed at the long run, and sometimes with conduct aimed at the short run (see p. 30). But those who aim at the short run when they could aim at the long run are inferior to those who aim at the long run, since (p. 31), in its higher stages, evolution takes place more and more by self-control, which is why (8.163) Henry James the elder was right in his very limited respect for morality, and why (6.440) to present a religious way of life as an ethical rule is to contract it. Christianity (1.675) sets duty (the merely ethical) at its proper finite figure.

At all times there have been people who thought that science and religion were in conflict with one another, and people who thought that they were not. In the later nineteenth century the controversy centered around evolution. Deniers of conflict had long used a distinction between true science and false science, and between genuine religion and spurious religion. In Huxley's version, the latter was a distinction between religion and theology; science, he said, was perfectly compatible with religion and at war only with theology. The same distinction was drawn, for example, by H. W. Beecher and by A. D. White.[14]

14. Thomas Henry Huxley, *Science and Hebrew Tradition, Collected Essays* (New York, 1897), *4*, 160–61; the passage was originally published in 1885. Henry Ward Beecher, *Evolution and Religion* (New York, 1885), p. 51. (Professor L. O. Mink called to my attention this place and Richard Hofstadter's discussion of it in his *Social Darwinism in American Thought* [Philadelphia, 1944], p. 15.) Andrew D. White, *History of the Warfare Between Science and*

Peirce as an American

It is clear that by the 1870s, if not earlier, Peirce had arrived at a similar view. Now the problem of defining the due and proper relation between religion and theology involves, and perhaps even coincides with, the problem of defining the due and proper relation between religion and science. I have already begun to explain why these two—religion and science—are for Peirce the fundamental approaches, routes, or avenues to reality. In trying to name what science and religion have in common, I have to devise a name of my own choosing, for Peirce has no fixed name of his own. (In 6.429 he does call them "species of reality.") In his system there is no category, no concept, that subsumes them both. Cassirer's concept of symbolic forms would be apropos; describing Peirce's system in Cassirer's terms, we would say that he recognizes two symbolic forms, the scientific and the religious.

SCIENCE AND RELIGION: THEIR RESPECTIVE MODES OF OPERATION

Peirce regards science and religion as two modes, and agents, of unification; his thought is incoherent to the extent that he does not depict the simultaneous, interlocking advance of the two unifications. But, filling in the blank in his canvas for him, we can say that he has two things in mind:

(1) Science achieves unification through inquiry. Inquiry is collaborative, communal; in order for it to progress, individuals must subjugate and sacrifice their individuality, e.g. they must (5.589 fin.) launch inquiries whose outcome they themselves will not live to see. Thus (7.87), scientists are like a colony of insects, "mere cells in a social organism" (1.647).

The reward for inquiry is collective. Scientists are approaching the exhaustion of knowledge in the sense that, though (1.405) there will never be a time when all truths are known, yet (8.12,

---

Theology (New York, 1896), Introduction. (Professor Perry Miller in a letter to me of November 26, 1951, contrasted the attitudes mirrored in the respective titles of White's book and of John William Draper's *History of the Conflict Between Religion and Science* [New York, 1875]. Professor Miller had previously made this point in lectures, as I was informed by Professor Murray Murphey.)

8.43–44) for every truth there is a time by which it will be known. (Note that this account conceives truth atomistically, rather than organically.) And (8.12, 8.43–44) a truth once known will stay known forever. "There may be questions concerning which the pendulum of opinion never would cease to oscillate. . . . But if so, those questions are *ipso facto* not *real* questions" (5.461). (Pragmatism can distinguish real questions from supposed questions [8.259, quoted below, p. 32].)

(2) Religion achieves unification in a way very different from science. The higher a religion the more catholic; Peirce, seeing resemblances between Buddhism and Christianity, thinks that by this test the Buddhisto-Christian religion is the highest one known so far. According to Peirce the central concept of Christianity is love. Whereas the way of science appears to consist of successive advances, with different methods and different parts, love does not appear to be broken up in this way.

We do not find any consecutive account of the modus operandi of love, but we can piece one together. The following is the merest sketch. Peirce's formula contains two parts: (1) assimilation of love to cognition, i.e. a sort of intellectualism, especially evident in his doctrine (1a) of viewpoints, (1b) of the pragmatic maxim, and (1c) of vagueness. But the intellectualism may also be seen in his account of egotism, that presents egotism as illogical. Besides the rationalistic or intellectualistic assimilation of love to cognition, there is also (2) an account of faith as akin to perception, yet also as like hope; here again the doctrine of vagueness is put to use.

A CRITIQUE OF THE SCIENTIFIC MODE

It is certain, Peirce says (5.587; 8.43; cf. 1.663; 5.408), that sooner or later the human race on earth will come to an end; but (8.43) also certain that living, minded things do or will exist elsewhere in the physical universe. Now it is understandable (though not plausible, because of the possible decay of civilization) that the truth once gained by mankind will never be lost again. It is not understandable how, if mankind should perish, truth hitherto gained would still be preserved for eternity.

Peirce as an American

But let us, to simplify the discussion, assume for the moment that the human race, subject to evolution, will go on forever. What might be hoped from our offspring and successors? Peirce's particular suggestion about the community of scientists is that it might serve as a model for the rest of the world. He gives some empirical evidence to show a correlation between scientific ability and high moral character. From this alleged correlation he infers the explanation that there is a General (in the metaphysical sense), or Universal, requisite for both scientific ability and moral goodness, to wit the quality of selflessness. Study of the advance of science can therefore throw light on the problem of how the moral order can advance.

In refutation of Peirce's argument I submit three considerations:

(1) As a norm, his ideal is noble; as a descriptive proposition, it overstates the facts of the case. Scientists, *qua* scientists, are not on the average so superior as Peirce makes them out to be.

(2) Even so far as his descriptive proposition is well-grounded, it is still not to the point, because the scientific community is self-selected; people not of a temperament to join this community don't join it. Now the hope that the scientific community would serve as a model is the hope that it would coincide with the human community. And this is the hope that there would be no people of a temperament that would lead them not to join the scientific community. But Peirce gives not the slightest support to this hope, nor is there any reason to share it. It could only happen by affecting reproduction and heredity in such a way that, after some time, people of a nonscientific temperament would not be generated. Peirce wants such a thing to be true, and so he favors a Lamarckian over a Darwinian theory of evolution; but even if evolution were Lamarckian, there would still remain in the realm of possibilities the unscientific personalities. Metaphysicians—both before and after Peirce—have tried to peg the realm of possibilities to the realm of actualities in such a way that there are no genuine, even though never actualized, possibilities. For my own part, I regard all such attempts as either unsuccessful or else true but trivial (true, by definition of 'genuine'); but in the present connection I will only remark that no such attempt is open to Peirce, because

of his doctrine of tychism. Conformity to law will never be perfect, and however much the scientific temperament may be the rule, chance exceptions to the rule will always occur. What needs to be shown is that these chance exceptions will not have a triggering effect in disrupting the scientific community.

(3) Even if the class of scientists coincided in extension with the class of human beings, there would still be a momentous intensional difference: the scientist, unless he is inhuman, is not merely and wholly a scientist.

This is not a point that Peirce overlooked. On the contrary, it is one he made much of, especially in his fin de siècle writings on theory versus practice. But he didn't bring it to bear on the present question. This is because he believed[15] that habits generalize.

Now the scientist must live and act, as well as theorize. Far from holding that the scientist must live by the light of his theory, Peirce gives elaborate reasons why he must cut off his practice from his theory, must set up a 'gulf' (Lieb, p. 6) between theory and practice. These reasons come down ultimately to two: (a) the theoretician may suspend belief indefinitely, whereas the practical man must act now; (b) in practical matters we have available a better guide than theory, namely instinct.

Peirce's defense of instinct—a defense original only in a few details, and very characteristic of its time—is Darwinian.[16]

One of these original details is Peirce's doctrine that we have right instincts for theorizing as well as for practical action. (This doctrine *relates* instinct to theory, without *identifying* the two.) Another is that these theorizing instincts, which take the special

15. For example in 7.256 he cites a case where training in visual perception improved auditory discrimination.

16. It belongs to what I have called, in the paper cited in n. 12 above, philosophical (rather than scientific) Darwinism. This is shown for example by the extrapolation mentioned in point (b) below (see p. 29). In keeping with philosophical Darwinism, Peirce understands 'instinct' in a sense generalized beyond ordinary usage. The generalization depends on assimilating native instinct ('nature' in a Greek sense) to acquired habit (which the Greeks called *second* nature). Only after such a generalization could Peirce think of saying (7.380–81) that instinct is higher and more developed than reason.

form of *guessing* instincts, are (7.380) halfway between infallibility and worthlessness.

I may briefly mention three objections to Peirce's defense of instinct: (a) In Bergson's version (*Creative Evolution*), the instincts that result from natural selection *substitute* for intelligence, they do not complement it. The vital need that they serve is clear. Peirce's version doesn't show (though 5.341 tries), as it should, that an instinct for quickly guessing the laws of nature is the sort of thing that would probably be developed by natural selection. (b) But in any case, Peirce extrapolates; he claims a validity for these instincts in all of philosophy, not just in that part which concerns the physical world. (c) The appeal to Darwinian natural selection here needs to be reconciled with Peirce's rejections of Darwinism elsewhere. A reconciliation is not out of the question, but it remains an agendum.

Besides giving an individual twist to the instinct theory, Peirce gives it a surprising lineage. This shows him in his role of synthesizing British with German philosophy. Although his instinct theory is much colored by Darwinism and by contemporary discussions, he himself traces it back to the Scottish common-sense philosophy, with its 'primary beliefs' or 'indubitables'. In his 1905 discussion of Critical Common-sensism (5.438–52) he explains both in what ways post-Darwinian results modify eighteenth-century beliefs and in what ways common-sensism must be made critical. 'Critical' means 'subjected to criticism' and especially to criticism in something like the Kantian sense. (Recall logic as 'the critic of arguments'.) So (5.482) Critical Common-sensism has a pedigree with two lineages—a British and a German ancestry.

Peirce contrasts theory and practice; what he means is not far from Husserl's concept of 'attitude', and we might well restate his doctrine as a contrast of the theoretical and the practical attitudes.[17] To some extent he founds ethics in the practical attitude. But (cf. pp. 23–24) there is another foundation, or

17. In 5.434 Peirce says that the practical attitude of the thinker to the past and to the future is different; in 5.589 he contrasts the practical with the scientific attitude.

ground, that plays a much larger part in his thinking—religion. Fundamentally, he derives ethical prescriptions from religion.

A word should be said about the gulf between theory and practice. To admit it, as to admit any gulf, is to go against the maxim of synechism. But sometimes this must be done. And if we look for the reasons for admitting this gulf, we will find one which is ineluctable. Theory is concerned with the long run; practice, with the short run. The gulf between them rests on the gulf between the long run and the short run, that is, between the whole infinite future and what will happen some finite time from now. But no gulf is more unbridgeable than the gulf between the infinite and the finite.

THE CHRISTIAN WAY

Now what is "the Christian theory of the way in which the world is to be made better and wiser" (7.274)?

The religious way and the Christian way will, as far as we can now see, coincide, for (Lieb, p. 28) "probably Christianity was a higher development out of Buddhism, modified by Jewish belief in a living God";[18] and (6.441–42) the fact that the gospel of love is also held by Buddhists, Confucians, etc. is in its favor: "The higher a religion, the more catholic." Now the reason why "a great catholic church is wanted" is that "without a church, the religion of love can have but a rudimentary existence" (6.443). And how may such a church universal be achieved? By right understanding together with self-control.

Existing partial churches can unite into a single universal church if obstacles to their doing so are removed. One obstacle is the divisiveness of creeds, which comes (cf. pp. 24–25) from failure to distinguish religion from theology. By historical and other arguments Peirce argues that, in an early period of decline, Christianity

18. A reference in this passage to W. B. Smith, *Der vorchristliche Jesus* (Giessen, 1906), implies that Smith's book was a source of this doctrine for Peirce. Is this the same Smith as the one to whom (Murphey, p. 15) Peirce wrote in 1908 an account of why he left the Unitarian for the Episcopal Church?

passed from a religion based on love to a theology based on hate (*odium theologicum*). The role of self-control is that, by deliberate exercise thereof, believers can give up insisting on their creeds and thus can weld themselves onto one another in spite of, because in disregard of, their credal differences. Now "in its higher stages, evolution takes place more and more largely through self-control" (5.433).

People who do not belong to one of the existing Christian churches can, by reflection, recognize their debt to Christian civilization (6.444), and the fact that faith sometimes goes unrecognized (Lieb, p. 27). Christianity is, in the last analysis, a hope, and (5.357) a hope which even the atheist, as his actions prove, shares. It must be as part of this project of making people aware of their own beliefs that Peirce wants (Lieb, p. 40) to show an all-reconciling point of view, an "enlargement of . . . horizon" (8.49). The religion of love can "be regarded in a higher point of view with St. John as the universal evolutionary formula" (6.441).

The higher point of view will enable us to surmount creeds, and thus to advance from theology to religion. In 1902 Peirce writes to William James (8.276), "Why don't you join the Church? Surely you won't allow metaphysical formulae, dead as the dust of the catacombs, to deprive you of your RIGHT to the influences of Church." Half a dozen years later, Peirce explains to a correspondent (Murphey, p. 15; cf. n. 18 above) that when he joined the Episcopal Church he did so without believing anything but the general essence and spirit of it. And writing in that same year of 1908 to Lady Welby, he tells her (Lieb, p. 28):

> I say the creed in church with the rest. By doing so I only signify, as I presume the majority do—and hope they do—my willingness to put aside, most heartily, anything that tends to separate me from my fellow Christians. For the very ground of my criticism of creeds [cf. 7.97 ff., of about this same period] is that every one of them was originally designed to produce such a separation, contrary to the notions of Him who said "He that is not against me is for me."

(Presumably Peirce means to be quoting Luke 9:50, "He that is not against us is for us"; compare Matthew 12:30, "He that is not with me is against me.")

By proposing as he does to discriminate what is the living, essential spirit in creeds from what is their dead, accidental body, Peirce may have in mind his Pragmatic Maxim, which was supposed to do just this kind of work, and which in his first extended statement of it— the *Popular Science Monthly* paper of 1878—was deliberately applied to a theological example, the doctrine of the Eucharist (5.401; cf. the retractation of 5.541). In the same context (5.402 n. 2) Peirce speaks of the Pragmatic Maxim as "the sole principle of logic which was recommended by Jesus" (in the teaching "By their fruits ye shall know them"); he might have mentioned also, as being in the same spirit, the Pauline counsel, "Prove all things; hold fast that which is good" (1 Thess. 5:21; cf. p. 16 above).

Now we may apply, as relevant to the present discussion, a remark of Peirce's to his fellow pragmatist James (8.259, a letter of 1904): "pragmatism solves no real problem [as characterized above, p. 26]. It only shows that supposed problems are not real problems." Most problems of theology, including those to which various creeds of Christendom committed themselves, would, Peirce no doubt believes, be exposed as pseudo-problems, and thus would be discarded from the essential living spirit of religion.

Pragmatism, then, will help people to understand the difference between accidental, private, idiosyncratic theology and common, public, essential religion. Complementary to pragmatism is the doctrine of fallibilism; and fallibilism is equally powerful in aiding religious unity through understanding. Fallibilism puts doubt in a man's mind that his own formulation of religious truth is utterly correct; one recalls Protestant arguments (such as Whichcote's) that defend religious tolerance on the ground of fallibilism.

Now fallibilism can be deduced from three propositions taken in conjunction: (1) a proposition is verified by its consequences; (2) the possible consequences are endless and the most we could even *hope* to do is to confirm the proposition with probability 1; and (3) probability 1 is not the same as certainty (1.141; cf. 1.88

and 5.24), because if the set of confirmations is infinite, no finite number of exceptions lowers the ratio from 1 to a proper fraction; thus there is no way of getting certainty.

Fallibilism, thus deduced, founds a deduction of its own: "The principle of continuity is the idea of fallibilism objectified" (1.171). Peirce must be thinking here, primarily if not solely, of continuity among human beings, that continuity which is gotten by their welding or melting themselves together; now if two people differ in religion, and each takes his fallibilism seriously and reflects, then the religious differences that separate him from the other man disappear, and the two individuals melt into continuity. "All communication from mind to mind is through continuity of being" (7.572). *In*fallibilism, on the other hand, leads (Lieb, p. 25) to *odium theologicum*.

Besides pragmatism and fallibilism, a third aspect of Peirce's logic is involved: the logic of vagueness, which, he says (5.506), he has worked out with something like completeness. He would no doubt have in mind, inter alia, the point (6.60, 6.65) that an explanation need not be perfectly precise; even (7.563–64) the basic doctrine of idealism itself, namely that to explain something is to "show how it traces its lineage to the womb of thought," does not admit of precise statement. And in particular, the idea that there is order in the universe (6.496) and (6.489, 6.505) the hypothesis of God are inherently vague. Precision, then, such as dogmas and creeds pretend to, would be *over*precision.

I believe that Peirce outrageously overworks his doctrine of vagueness, but I shall not present my reasons in this paper, for a deeper-cutting criticism must claim priority. Peirce purports to be showing a *way;* and it is not enough to show a way in which unification *can* or *may* come about. What we would above all prefer is a way in which it *surely will.* Peirce gives a reason why our first preference is too strong, because inherently unsatisfiable: it is deterministic, and determinism is radically unreasonable. Let us grant his point and settle for his own lesser demand—that one may reasonably call for a way in which unification will *tend* to come about.

Peirce often claims to be giving reasons (of diverse cogency) for believing that there is such a tendency. A book could (and perhaps will) be written about these reasons; but, to be brief, a feature that they all have in common is that he himself, in other discussions, undermines them all.

For example, he says in a passage quoted earlier (p. 31) that evolution in its higher stages operates more and more through self-control. He leaves it unjustifiably vague whether this means, as regards the human race, that an increasing proportion of human beings *will* exercise self-control in matters of religion. I say he leaves this unjustifiably vague; but actually it doesn't matter in the least. For (5.408, 5.587) sooner or later the human race will come to an end, and any self-controlling that is done after that will be done by whatever other minds there are in the universe. (In 5.485 *fin.* Peirce provides for other than human finite minds by distinguishing psychics from psychology, but he does not ordinarily make use of this distinction.)

In addition, if the human race lasts long enough before its extinction, it will likely have evolved into something else; the 1877 article on "The Fixation of Belief" grounded what *ought* to be on what *is* (or *will be*), but its *is* was the de facto *is* of present human nature, as Peirce subsequently realized (5.28). We observe here a type of inconsistency into which Peirce is continually falling. Now he expands his horizon, now he contracts it; Peirce's reader must always ask himself what horizon Peirce has set in any given discussion. Shortly after the remark (5.506) that he has worked out the logic of vagueness, he alleges (5.509) that the list of indubitable propositions is more or less the same for all men; and this, though a statement of his ripest years (ca. 1905) speaks as though evolution of man into something other than man need not be contemplated as a possibility.

PEIRCE'S GREAT HOPE (5.407)

Various philosophers have spoken of the presuppositions made by logic, by inductive reasoning especially (cf. 6.100; 2.777), but also by inquiry in general. And, somewhat differently, philosophers

Peirce as an American

(especially Germans, e.g. 3.432) have spoken of the presuppositions of this or that science, or of thought in general, or of experience (3.635).

In the first place, Peirce objects (5.382 n.; cf. 6.39) to the word 'presupposition' itself as a rendering of German *Voraussetzung*, on the ground that the latter was instituted to render in German the Greek and Latin terms traditionally rendered in English by *postulate*.

More deeply, Peirce attacks claims that 'postulate' means something special or recondite. He says (6.39, 6.612) that to postulate something is simply to hope that it is true, or to *presume* it. Now in 2.774, 2.776 presumption is expressly identified with abduction (alias retroduction and hypothesis), which helps us to determine more precisely what Peirce means. Neither we nor he would call every hypothesis a hope, and somewhere the difference between the two has gotten lost. Rather similar to *pre*suming is *as*suming; 2.29 tells us that "a reasonable disputant disputes because he hopes, or at least, goes upon the assumption that the dispute will come to something."

We have come across cases before where Peirce holds in one context a view he derides in another. His view of postulates has aspects of being another such case. He is known for his view that induction needs no special justification (1.608; 6.41–42, 6.100, 6.410; cf. 5.342) because (1.608) its success is conditional; he similarly (2.777, 2.786) justifies 'presumption' (hypothesis) on the ground that it will work if any method will. Now whenever we do presume (hypothesize), we thereby make also the 'primary hypothesis' (7.220) that the human mind has a natural affinity for the truth. And this would be a German-type postulate.

Also, whenever Peirce speaks of maxims (he repeatedly insists that Pragmatism is a maxim), aren't these maxims virtually the same as regulative principles, or postulates?

Perhaps the difference that Peirce has in mind is shown by 3.215, which says that "Kant's distinction of regulative and constitutive principles is unsound." It is the *distinction* that is unsound, in treating them as two different *kinds* of principles; for one of the presumptions of logic is (2.646; cf. 7.463 concerning a particular instance) the synechistic presumption that differences are differences of degree.

In addition to the primary hypothesis of logic, there are "three sentiments" which (2.655) are "indispensable requirements of logic," all of them involving an indefinitely continuing community of inquirers. These three sentiments respectively resemble charity, faith, and hope.

What Peirce understands by 'hope' is further clarified by 2.113: logic warrants only a *hope,* not a *belief,* that such and such will be so. Namely (6.189), we suppose, or hope, that our logic corresponds to the logic exhibited by the world that we study. Again, Peirce uses the concept of hope in defending against Royce his concept of law as *would-be* thus (8.113), that to say how things would be, in the infinitely long run, is to say how we hope they will be.

For Peirce is an optimist. He is at pains to argue (6.484; cf. 1.405; I have simplified his argument) that optimism is the normal and pessimism an abnormal human condition; and even though logic is guided by the rule of hope (1.405), we are (5.366) all of us, even the atheist, more hopeful than logic would warrant (5.357), for we are infinitely hopeful.

To my mind, it is a disappointment to recede from an assurance to a hope. But from Peirce's point of view, the recession is a gain, because it aids the work of unification. Science and religion, knowledge and faith come closer together when both are seen to have the same foundation, namely hope. When Peirce finds analogues in logic for charity, faith, and hope, this sounds fanciful, and is, in truth, somewhat strained; but it represents a genuine endeavor and a genuine inquiry, not a merely mechanical application of his principles.

William Cullen Bryant, in stanza 9 of "The Battle Field," says:

> Truth, crushed to earth, shall rise again
> Th'eternal years of God are hers
> But error, wounded, writhes in pain
> And dies among his worshipers.

Peirce as an American

Peirce was fond of this passage, which he cites (5.408) shortly after having spoken (5.407) of "this great hope" about the fated truth (cf. 5.582 on the fated truth), and which he cites in three other places—1.217, 7.325, and Lieb, p. 26. (In two of these places he attributes it to Pope.) He liked the quatrain because it gave poetic expression to his favorite tenet that truth has a greater tendency than falsehood to be believed (5.431), and will, sooner or later, prevail. That he cannot say *anything* about when this 'sooner or later' will be is another aspect of the fact that his tenet is a hope, not a piece of knowledge nor even a belief.

SUMMARY

Instead of retracing the steps of my argument just as I gave them, I think it will be clearer if I state the leading thoughts in a different order.

(1) The great American achievement is political: an act of voluntary, communal, self-controlled self-unification.

(2) This political achievement *illustrates* what Peirce regards as the general formula of the evolutionary good.

(3) Peirce is not a political philosopher, and America has not in general been outstanding for its contributions to philosophy. Nevertheless, Peirce, an outstanding philosopher, develops a philosophy of which the outstanding American achievement is an instance. He gives a philosophical rationale for what is best in America; and in this respect, in addition to being an American and a philosopher, he deserves to be called an American philosopher.

(4) And moreover, Peirce sets himself to accomplishing in philosophy something like the political unification of the states. He tries to unify two sets of ideas; inasmuch as these sets are associated, contingently, with two nations, the British and the German, it is not surprising if the unifier himself belongs to neither of these nations, and yet feels a sympathy with both.

(5) But it might seem that the parallel between politics and philosophy fails in that the American political unification was autonomous and internal, whereas so far as Peirce the philosoph-

ical unifier is neither British nor German, he is external to what he unifies and the unification is imposed from without. I imagine that Peirce would reply to this objection as follows: Peirce's method is external only so far as one or the other method resists criticism. Criticism is his fundamental method, and so far as the ideas to be unified submit to criticism, the unification that will surely result from the criticism is of their own making.

(6) Peirce himself stands in need of criticism, and the criticism I have made of him is a very serious one. This is that, William Cullen Bryant notwithstanding, we have absolutely no assurance that truth will prevail and that unification does tend to come about. My criticism has shown that Peirce expressed himself misleadingly, and that what he at first blew up into a 'demonstration' shrank to a conviction and finally shriveled to a hope. In entertaining this hope, Peirce recognized himself as an optimist.

(7) I will let Peirce have the last word. Even though Americans are often thought to be optimistic, and may in certain matters be more optimistic than the Old World, still Peirce would claim that optimism is seated in human, and not just in American, nature; and the role of the American optimist would be, at most, to awaken the rest of the world to self-knowledge.

APPENDIX: WELDING

The welding metaphor describes a process by comparing it to a process in which substances become parts of substances. The things that are thus compared with substances are mostly (a) human individuals and (b) feelings and ideas. The metaphor applies equally, though much less frequently, to (c) other things, such as the points of space and the instants of time.

One step of the argument in Peirce's philosophy assimilates (a) to (b): says that human beings are signs and signs are living and mindlike things. "Man's glassy [i.e. mirrorlike] essence" (6.238–71) argues this step (see also 5.314; 6.155, 6.344).

But another step in Peirce's philosophy argues that man is not perfectly and actually a sign; and a human being is an individual so far as he falls short of being a sign.

38

Peirce as an American

Peirce uses a number of other words with approximately the same force as the intransitive or reflexive verb 'weld': 'merge' (1.164; 5.204), 'flow' (1.39), 'melt' (5.204), and 'coalesce' (5.4). These latter, with their liquid- or fluid-metaphor, are more apt than 'weld' when Peirce wants to emphasize the active spontaneity of the things welding, and when (5.402 n. 2) he wants to stress that "every point directly partakes the being of every other"; the welding metaphor is apter when he wishes to emphasize the solidity of the product, the welded iron block. The manner in which literal welding is done—application of intense external heat to cause temporary liquefaction—is irrelevant to the purpose of the metaphor. What is relevant is the change from some heap of solids into some continuous, single solid. I conjecture the historical explanation that Peirce used the welding metaphor so much because the technique of welding iron and steel was new and spectacular in his day.

Another equivalent of intransitive 'weld' is the colorless phrase "come into relation" (6.199).

The intransitive and reflexive senses of 'weld' and the other verbs serve very well to express continuity, but precisely because they don't imply an external agent, they don't very well serve to express Thirdness. This is the role of the verb 'weld' used transitively. All triadic relations involve welding (1.363 n.). Peirce uses "bridge over [a gulf, chasm]," "bring into relation" (both 1.359), and "connect" (6.143) in an approximately equivalent way. And 6.262 speaks, in a certain connection, of "the only bridge that can span the chasm."

Individuals are individuated by ignorance and error (5.233–35, 5.283, 5.317), which (1.673) is the same as their blind will; individuals are enjoined (1.629, 1.673) to weld themselves together by self-immolation, also called self-abnegation. This is the injunction of religion (1.673) as well as of logic (5.354–56). Every sign welds into one the two quasi-minds that interpret it (4.551). In another way, the Church welds its members together into a common perception of the Glory of the Highest (6.429).

Besides individuals, feelings and ideas are welded. Habit (6.585), association (6.137, 6.143 fin.), and reflection (6.612) weld feelings.

It is chiefly human beings that weld ideas. The scientist must weld his idioscopic findings to cenoscopy (7.87); in 6.2, cenoscopy welds itself to idioscopy. Some attempts at welding one idea to another are grotesque (5.503) or vain (5.12), like Chauncey Wright's attempt to weld Darwin's ideas to Mill's. But when an attempt at welding is successful, we can (6.181) enter into another person's point of view by welding our reasonings to his. Peirce writes in 1909 to Lady Welby (Lieb, p. 40) that an all-reconciling point of view can be found and shown. Perhaps this is St. John's gospel of love, which, "regarded in a higher point of view" (6.441), is "the universal evolutionary formula."

As to how to weld ideas to ideas, the way is shown by mathematics, of which (6.30; cf. 1.354 section 7.3, and 1.400) "metaphysics has always been the ape." Modern geometry, for instance, by its "bridging over of the innumerable distinct cases with which the ancient science was encumbered" (1.359), effects a unification and an advance; and (1.82) subsequent geometry has advanced beyond Descartes in this respect.

One of the most fruitful methods in the advance of science is (2.110; 6.460; 7.66, 7.81) adapting methods from one science to another. Adaptation of inductive generalizations from one science to another is often mentioned by philosophers under the name Aristotle gives to it: *metabasis eis allo genos* [transfer to another genus]. In effect, Peirce is proposing for methods an analogue to metabasis of inductions. Adaptation is, one gathers from Peirce's remarks, one of the techniques of welding available to the scientist (and, in general, to the man who works with ideas). "If there be no true continuous growth in men's ideas, where else in the world should it be looked for?" (1.40). And (2.157) this growth is effected "by . . . each researcher's . . . joining his own work in one continuous piece to that already done."

One topic leads into another. The topic of continuous growth in ideas leads into the topic of how it is that Peirce at times speaks in a contrary way, as if the major advances in science were cataclysmic. That is a topic for some other paper; since (in brief) his view is that advance in retroduction is cataclysmic, whereas in induction it is continuous and cumulative; the topic of dealing with those places where Peirce stresses cataclysm would pertain to a discussion of retroduction.

In welding ideas, as in welding human individuals, self-immolation of the welder may be needed; if so, let the selves to be immolated murmur "Blessed are we" (1.670). This injunction has the sanction not only of religion but (5.354–56) also of logic.

Peirce's concept of welding welds religion not only to logic but also to mathematics. "The very supreme commandment of sentiment is that man should generalize, or what the logic of relatives shows to be the same thing, should become welded into the universal continuum" (1.673). But generalization is a fundamental technique of mathematics (1.83; 4.116–18; 6.26), and (3.451, 3.514, 3.520, all contra Schröder) mathematics shows by examples that generalization is something to be achieved, not something to be claimed at the outset.

So much for the welding of (a) human individuals and of (b) feelings and ideas. As for (c) space and time, are they welders or the results of welding? Whichever they are, the result is that continuity involves welding (6.168 *fin.*). In 4.172 the common view that—to restate it in Peirce's metaphor—they are welders is rejected as a *hysteron proteron*. In 5.204–05 he speaks of their merging, flowing, melting (all in the intransitive and reflexive versions). In 6.330, time and space weld impulses together. Perhaps Peirce's definitive view would be that space and time, themselves the results of welding (suggested as a possibility in 6.191), in turn function as welders.

Chapter 2 Notes Toward a Logic of Discovery

Norwood Russell Hanson

I Suppose Charles Sanders Peirce were alive today. He would now see some of his ideas being rejected just as energetically as they were fifty years ago. Consider his idea of 'A Logic of Discovery'. The historian of science in him always caught fire when contemplating the contexts within which new discoveries were conceived. As a philosopher of science Peirce longed to understand the errant reasoning which heralded such discoveries—some of them the greatest moments in the entire history of ideas. How then to characterize the perplexed reflections of scientific discoverers? How to formulate the criteria in terms of which one innovator might be said to have 'reasoned well' while groping towards 'the unprecedented'—while others reasoned poorly? How to scan, with the eye of a logician, the tortuous trails traversed by creative intellects? How to scribble down the first few pages of what might ultimately be called "A Logic of Discovery"?

With this set of leading questions Peirce soon lost most of his high-collared, button-shoed audience. But so also would he lose most open-collared, sandal-shod audiences today—for the very words 'logic of discovery' seem not to fit together; at their mention philosophers scurry for cover, they claw the auditorium walls, or chew the college carpets in sophisticated, seething incredulity and disdain.

Thus Karl Popper pronounces: "the act of conceiving . . . a theory, seems to me neither to call for logical analysis nor to be susceptible of it."[1] And "there is no such thing as a logical method

1. K. R. Popper, *The Logic of Scientific Discovery* (London, 1959), p. 31.

of having new ideas, or a logical reconstruction of this process."[2] Hans Reichenbach ruled that philosophers of science "cannot be concerned with [reasons for suggesting hypotheses], but only with [reasons for accepting hypotheses]."[3] Richard Braithwaite elaborates: "The solution of these historical problems involves the individual psychology of thinking and the sociology of thought. None of these questions are our business here."[4] In every line he wrote about 'scientific explanation' Peirce signaled that the conceptual analysis of discovery *was* his business—indeed, his philosophical duty. Thus my conjecture that he would again be swimming against the professional academic stream even in our 1960s—every bit as much as he had done in the 1890s.

Two possible judgments concerning this snap forth:

(1) Peirce still is, as he always was, behind the times in his writings. Or,

(2) we are still not ready for much of Peirce's philosophy—no more than were our grandparents.

I shall opt for the second of these judgments, that Peirce remains far ahead of us. Still, I will place the responsibility for this 'breakdown in communications' at the tip of Peirce's own penpoint. We have trouble getting clear about his 'philosophy of discovery' just because he was not clear about much of it himself. I'll do my best to render his considerable insights defensible against today's torpedoes of critical analysis.

II   Let's get one thing straight. When Popper, Reichenbach, Braithwaite, and others argue that there is no logical analysis appropriate to the intricate and mysterious psychological complex within which new ideas spark forth, they are saying nothing of which Peirce was unaware. He urges that "knowledge of the processes of thinking [even were it at hand] . . . would be entirely irrelevant to . . . knowledge of the nature of our reasonings"

2. Ibid., p. 32.
3. H. Reichenbach, *Experience and Prediction* (Chicago, 1948), p. 382.
4. R. B. Braithwaite, *Scientific Explanation* (Cambridge, 1953), pp. 20–21.

(2.185). The philosopher is properly concerned only with the formal relationship between the initiation of a problem and its solution (2.27). Peirce was as capable as are our ultramodern contemporaries of detecting a genetic fallacy. So also had been John Stuart Mill when he wrote: "There is no science which will enable a man to bethink himself of that which will suit his purpose."[5] Aristotle himself, the original student of 'a logic of discovery',[6] knew well the objections to offering factual histories of how things actually happened in response to requests for philosophical analysis of why things must be thought of just so in order to be thought of coherently *at all*. 'The Logic of X' can never be identical with 'The Recipe For Making X'—or with 'The History of X', or with 'The Psychology of X'. A fortiori 'A Logic of Discovery' could hardly be taken by a thinker of Peirce's stature to be 'A Manual For Making Discoveries', or 'A History of Great Discoveries', or 'A Psychological Sketch of Discoverers'.

That Aristotle, Bacon, Mill, Whewell, Schiller, and Peirce knew so well the differences between recipes, histories, psychology, *and logic*—and yet still wrote of 'a logic of discovery'—this should suggest a modicum of caution against rejecting wholesale *any* such notion on the grounds that it can only be psychology, sociology or history. Peirce denied just this; but none are so deaf as those who will not hear! Today's most influential analytical philosophers will not listen to Peirce on this. All the more, then, must we argue his thesis carefully and sympathetically, yet strictly and without compromise.

III   Aristotle[7] and Peirce (1.188) both suggested that there may be more for a philosopher of science to do than just analyze the completed arguments supporting already formed hypotheses. F. C. S. Schiller also distinguished 'The Logic of Proof' from 'The Logic of Discovery',[8] even though he was merely expressing

---

5. J. S. Mill, *A System of Logic* (London, 1843), Bk. III, Ch. 1.
6. Aristotle, *Posterior Analytics*, Bk. II, Ch. 19; *Prior Analytics*, Bk. II, Ch. 25.
7. Ibid.
8. F. C. S. Schiller, "The Logic of Discovery," *Studies in the History and Methods of the Sciences*, ed. Charles Singer (2 vols. Oxford, 1917–1921).

Notes Toward a Logic of Discovery

exasperation with his syllogism-sectioning colleagues; the attention now accorded to inductive reasoning, probability, and the principles of theory construction—this would have gone far to satisfy Schiller.

But not Peirce. Books like *Logik der Forschung, Experience and Prediction,* and *Scientific Explanation* would have seemed to Peirce more concerned with a 'Logic of Finished Research Reports' than with discovery. Such modern works consider how to set out reasons in support of hypotheses once they are well-formulated and explicitly proposed. These books do not, however, treat of the conceptual context within which such hypotheses are initially conceived and entertained—within which, indeed, *Forschung,* experience, and explanation really affect the pulse of the body scientific.

Peirce insisted that the original formulation of an hypothesis H, and the decision seriously to entertain H, can be a wholly reasonable undertaking. There may be good reasons, or poor ones, for suggesting one kind of hypothesis initially, rather than some wholly different kind.

IV   We are already close to distinguishing:

(1) reasons for accepting an hypothesis, H, from
(2) reasons for entertaining H in the first place.

Most philosophers today, such as Herbert Feigl, deny any logical difference between (1) and (2). This denial will be 'Peirce-d' in due course. But surely one's reasons for accepting an H are just those reasons one has for thinking H to be *true.* And is it not equally clear that one might have reasons for entertaining some H seriously long before having reason for taking H to be true?

[At this very moment, 6:30 A.M. on July 31, 1964, 'Ranger 7' is rocketing toward the moon—shortly to send us close-up TV pictures of the lunar surface. But now, three hours before the first picture-signal is shot back to us, we have excellent reasons for entertaining this following H: that the moon's surface is a dead, pocked, dust-covered rock-crust. Later on we'll have strong reasons for asserting or denying that H.]

Who denies that there is *some* difference between such sets of reasons?

> But is it a difference that makes any difference? [Feigl would ask.] Our reasons for now construing H as a *plausible conjecture* may indeed differ somehow from our later reasons for taking H as confirmed. But this is not a difference in type; initially we indulge in guesswork among inconclusive, spotty data. Finally we can enjoy reliable inference from well-marshaled evidence. The discoverer's reasoning, then, ranges over a spectrum of factual support—beginning in inadequate, ill-arrayed data and coming to rest in abundant, well-diversified evidence buttressed by batteries of beautiful theories. The difference between reasons for entertaining H and reasons for accepting H is one of degree only—not of logical type at all. What we lack in respectable evidence at first, we make up in intuition, hunches and experiential frosting—the functions of which are a matter of psychological fact, not logic or analysis.

This hypothetical Feiglean missile lands squarely on the mark. Let's recoil into a distinction.[9] Our original division between

(1) reasons for accepting H, and
(2) reasons for entertaining H,

must now be reset in more guarded language. Distinguish now

(1′) reasons for accepting some particular, minutely detailed, and uniquely specified H from
(2′) reasons for suggesting that, whatever specific claim the

---

9. It's a distinction I've drawn before, often; see "The Logic of Discovery," *Journal of Philosophy*, 55 (1958), 1073–1089; "More on 'The Logic of Discovery'," *Journal of Philosophy*, 57 (1960), 182–88; "Is There a Logic of Discovery?" *Current Issues in the Philosophy of Science,* ed. H. Feigl and G. Maxwell (New York, 1961), pp. 20–35, 40–42; "Retroductive Inference," *Philosophy of Science, The Delaware Seminar,* ed. Bernard Baumrin (2 vols. New York, 1961–63), *1,* 21–37; "The Idea of a Logic of Discovery," *forthcoming* in *Dialogue.*

> successful H may be discovered to make, it will nonetheless be an H of one *kind* rather than any other.[10]

Aristotle never sought this distinction on these grounds. Peirce seems often to grope for it; thus he writes of the puzzling out of an hypothesis-type that "it is very little hampered by logical rules, nevertheless [it] is logical inference . . . having a perfectly definite logical form" (5.188).

In earlier papers I sought to distinguish between reasons for accepting particular Hs and reasons for entertaining H-types.[11] But with even this little laid bare it already appears that different ingredients have long been lumped into the idea of a 'Logic of Discovery'. Each of these is present in Peirce, somewhere. And each of them has figured somewhere in my own past scribblings.[12] I will dub these ingredients:

(A) 'Logic of Discovery' à la *Patterns of Discovery*
(B) 'Logic of Discovery' à la *Is There A Logic of Discovery?*
(C) 'Logic of Discovery' à la *Retroductive Inference*.[13]

This, for no reason better than that the conceptual strands later to be intertwined are best known to me in these terms. If *per*

---

10. Thus inspection of Ranger's TV signals may give us reasons for accepting or rejecting some particular H describing the fine-scale lunar topography, e.g. that the 'Seas' are leagues-deep in dust. But even now (7 A.M.) before the first such signal arrives, we have the best reasons for doubting that Ranger's cameras will disclose Italianate rococo tracery in the lunar rockeries, or meringue froth-work in the Mare Nubium, or Edelweiss along the Apennines. The ultimately successful H, we may even now reason, will not be of a type concerned with botanical description, human handiwork, or even physical foment. Our reasons for these expectations are inductively inconclusive, perhaps. But, resting (as they do) on largely analogical considerations, their evaluation cannot be as is that obtaining for our reasons for accepting some 'successful' H *as true* (e.g. that the lunar crust is rocky and exposed, and not all buried in dust, an H articulated after the pictures are 'in').

11. Cf. "The Logic of Discovery," and "Is There a Logic of Scientific Discovery?"

12. The classification originates with my student, C. T. Warner.

13. *Patterns of Discovery* (Cambridge, 1958); "Is There a Logic of Scientific Discovery?"; "Retroductive Inference."

impossibile Peirce should one day have to write about *my* 'philosophy of discovery' he may feel equally free to instantiate (A), (B), and (C) with quiddities from his own quill.

V   (A) In *Patterns of Discovery* (henceforth *PD*) 'explaining x' is represented as 'setting x into a conceptual framework'. *Discovery* is thus characterized as 'the dawning of an aspect of x' such that x is at last seen as part of a more comprehensive and comprehensible pattern; earlier, x might have been anomalous in seeming not to fit any intelligible organization of ideas. Now, the factual details of discovery constitute a subject matter for psychology—wherein words like 'intuition', 'insight', 'hunch', 'in a flash', etc., are descriptively associated with the phenomenon to be investigated. But *that* such spectacular reorganizations of concepts do occur is a matter of profound epistemological importance. *PD* traced some philosophical implications of such sudden *coagula* in the data of scientific perception. There, retroduction was remarked as the grounding discoverers give to individual anomalies—thereby rendering them nonproblematic, nonanomalous, *explained*. Peirce probes all this in many places (2.624, 2.638–39, 5.183, 5.591).

(B) In "Is There A Logic of Scientific Discovery?" (henceforth LSD) 'having reasons for entertaining possible explanations of x' is represented as 'considering that the explanation of x will be of one *type,* rather than some other'. This was discussed above. Peirce pieced together pertinent parts of this position (5.196).

(C) In "Retroductive Inference" (henceforth RI) 'having found an explanation of x' was represented as 'having reasoned one's way back from an encountered anomaly up to top-of-the-page *explicantia*'. As Peirce often noted, when logical rules are incorporated into practice, they do not cease being logical for that reason (2.181, 2.589, 2.650). So then, also, if the *finished* explanation of x exfoliates quasideductively from 'high level hypotheses' down through a theoretical inference-network, terminating ultimately in a 'lowlevel' description of x—then something resembling that same inference-network must have been traversed by the scientist who, when perplexed by x, did seek to 'explain it' by reasoning his way (and x's) back up into a 'control-tower' of unchallengeable commitments. The x is rendered nonanomalous when set 'as a matter of course' (Peirce's favorite phrase) into the framework of what was initially given as clearly understood. Of this reasoning-pattern more will follow; Peirce wrote much (2.183, 2.623–24, 2.638–39; 6.12).

VI   My objective is to locate a philosophically reasonable designatum for the expression 'A Logic of Discovery'. This involves composing a sort of three-part Fugue, each line of which is sung out somewhere in Peirce's *Collected Papers*—sometimes fortissimo and with resounding clarity, sometimes obscurely and sotto voce. Each theme is also discussed somewhere in my scribblings during the past decade—but again, as with Peirce, the three parts are discussed quite independently and without harmonization between parts. Can the 'Logics of Discovery' à la (A) *PD,* (B) LSD and (C) RI be composed so as to form one consonant, harmonious, well formed entity for philosophical inquiry? Peirce never undertook to do this, alas. His faithful readers have had to take much on faith. Yet interrelating (A), (B), and (C) *must* be undertaken if 'The Logic of Discovery' is ever to be understood as being other than

(a) 'A Laboratory Manual For Otherwise Incompetent Scientists' on the one hand, or
(b) 'A Logician's Symbolic Restatement of The Historical and Psychological Conditioning of Great Discoveries' on the other.

With this much as our Introductory Toccata then, let us structure the three Peirce-Hanson 'discovery-themes' (if such a bipartite reference is not too presumptuous) into one full philosophical Fugue—all in answer to the Kapell-meister's leading motif-question:

WHAT WOULD A 'LOGIC OF DISCOVERY' BE ABOUT?

The better to structure what follows I'll supply the dénouement at once, by the principle 'Answer now, argue later'.

49

A Logic of Discovery should concern itself with the scientists' actual reasoning which

    C. proceeds retroductively, *from an anomaly* to
    B. the delineation of a *kind* of explanatory H which
    A. fits into an organized *pattern* of concepts.

The C-B-A ordering of this 'answer' indicates that my own studies, from *PD* through LSD to RI most recently, have proceeded from general to more particular aspects of discovery. Here, however, we must proceed in reverse, discussing first the *occasion* for scientific inquiry and *retroductive inference* therefrom.

VII   *The* insight of the hypothetico-deductive analysis (henceforth HD) turns on distinguishing the rational activity of mathematicians from that of natural scientists. Popper, Reichenbach, Braithwaite—Carnap, Feigl, Bergmann—draw this distinction better than did earlier inductive logicians like Hume, Mill, Jevons, Venn, and Johnson. Mathematicians argue 'typically' when they entertain premisses solely to 'unpack' them. Their concern is neither with the truth-or-falsity of the premisses, nor with that of the conclusions unpackable therefrom. The 'unpacking relationship' alone is what interests the formal scientist. The natural scientist, however, cares not only about consistency within arbitrary universes of discourse; he is concerned also with the contingent truth of claims about *the* universe—the one in which we live. That a statement follows from *some* premiss cluster may be a necessary condition for its descriptive utility. But it is not sufficient. False conclusions can follow validly from factually false premisses, or from logically false ones.

If each premiss is contingently true, and if the deduction is valid, the conclusion will have 'about' the same probability as its premisses.

But problems seldom come to the scientist thus. Rarely is he provided with a list of probably-true claims and charged to draw up another list of their consequences. Usually he encounters some

Notes Toward a Logic of Discovery

anomaly; he desires an explanation of it.[14] It cannot follow obviously from any obvious premiss cluster; for, in such a case, it would not be anomalous—it would not constitute a perplexing occasion for further inquiry. So, one proceeds to cluster some established general truths with hypotheses about particular events, to see whether they may not jointly entail the anomaly.

But now, after the injection of hypotheses, now estimate the probability: this is much more difficult. The anomaly's description is assumed to be correct. The available premisses obtain. From the joint probability of the anomaly, plus the confirmed general premisses, one now seeks to estimate the probability of an hypothesis which (when conjoined with the premisses), *entails* the anomaly. This is an intricate and challenging determination—much more so than in the more 'orthodox' situation of estimating the probabilities of expected (nonanomalous) conclusions as inferred from familiar premisses whose probabilities are already estimated.

The HD account, then, is concerned not only with *conclusion deducing,* but with *hypothesis testing.* Hypotheses, as just suggested, are tested by linking them with already confirmed statements to form a sort of premiss cluster. From this cluster observational consequences are generated (ideally) by straightforward deductive inference. If these are confirmed in observation, the hypothesis is to that extent confirmed also. This is the very meaning of 'having good reasons for accepting H'. But if further consequences turn out to be observationally false, the probability of the hypothesis diminishes accordingly. And *that* is the meaning of '*not* having good reasons for accepting H'.

Much scientific reasoning and argumentation displays this HD pattern—perhaps more than the critics of HD analysis realize, although perhaps not as much as HD enthusiasts suppose. Whenever the extension of a partially confirmed theory is in question, one deductively generates further observational consequences of the theory—initially unsuspected, perhaps—and checks these

14. How like Aristotle's pronouncement "All knowledge begins in astonishment." And how like hundreds of things said by John Dewey in e.g. *How We Think; Logic: The Theory of Inquiry,* etc.

against the facts. Indeed, detecting flaws in apparatus, and deviations in measuring instruments—as well as happening upon the 'theoretical discovery' of wholly unexpected phenomena (such as Dirac's positron)—consists largely in deductively decomposing the premiss clusters of theoretical science. This sets out the 'logical expectations' of a given theory (an infinitely wider class than its 'psychological expectations'), and hence highlights any factual deviation from these expectations. The very identification of an event as 'anomalous' depends on some such HD elaboration of familiar premiss clusters. For we could not be perplexed by Nature save when She does the unexpected; but we cannot know what *counts* as 'unexpected' until we have some fairly full theories whose consequences *constitute* our expectations! So, in a sense, the very rationale behind 'expectation' is of the HD form, and there could be no occasion for factual inquiry without knowledge structured in that form.

The HD theorist attends thus to the scientist's inferences from contingent premiss clusters to observationally vulnerable conclusions, *all* of them—the psychologically *and* the logically expected ones.

The Retroductive Account (henceforth RD), however, focuses rather on the explanation of anomalies—those conclusions which, although logically 'expected', are psychologically quite unexpected. RD enthusiasts think scientific argumentation to consist primarily in the recognition of anomalies, and then in the subsequent search for some premiss cluster which, if confirmed, would 'explain' the anomaly—i.e., by entailing it (at least that) as the 'previous' theory may not have done. This premiss cluster will contain initial conditions and an hypothesis, the form of which may sometimes 'reveal itself' (psychologically) by its initial absence from the cluster.[15]

15. Thus, that the Law of Universal Gravitation had an inverse square *form* seemed clear to the young Newton (in 1665) from the 'logical gap' left in the cluster of known mechanical laws when he assumed that such laws were sufficient to explain *all* mechanical phenomena (the tides, hydrodynamics, ballistics, celestial motions, etc.). Some further hypothesis was needed. But although *it* was not discovered in all its particulars until 1687, Newton perceived its form

Notes Toward a Logic of Discovery

So, while the HD account usually pictures the scientist with a ready-made theory (replete with established hypotheses) and a vast store of initial conditions in hand—deductively generating testable observation statements from these—the RD account pictures him only as possessing the initial conditions and some profoundly upsetting anomaly, by reflections upon which he seeks an hypothesis, or rather a *kind* of hypothesis, to explain the anomaly and to found a new theory. That is, he seeks a novel HD framework within which to reveal the anomaly as logically-to-be-expected. Again, the HD account focuses on *hypothesis testing* after the Hs are fully formed (e.g. the Law of Universal Gravitation as construed *after* 1687 when being systematically tested by Halley, Lagrange, Clairault, Euler, Gauss, Laplace, and Leverrier); the RD account is concerned with *anomaly explaining*—this is 'hypothesis forming', during which time even the *type* of explanation may remain unsettled (e.g. the Law of Universal Gravitation as construed before 1665 when being debated, speculated about, and hammered out by Borelli, Wren, Barrow, and Hooke).

Some signal events have involved reasoning of this RD variety. The discovery of Neptune (by Adams and Leverrier) *via* the Inverse Problem of Perturbations,[16] and of the Neutrino—these are surely characterizable thus. Just as the discovery of Pluto, and of the Antiproton, seem somehow much better described in HD terms. For here one runs out, or 'unpacks', the consequences of an accepted theory and tests them observationally. In the RD case, however, some facts surprisingly *fail* to confirm the consequences of an accepted theory; one then undertakes to argue *from* these to some new hypothesis, or hypothesis-kind, which ultimately may resolve the anomaly.

'lurking' in the very statement of his problem in 1665. He was then prepared to forecast what *type* of hypothesis would answer his general problem. Even then, in 1665, he could have given good reasons for anticipating that the ultimately successful hypothesis would be of the $1/r^2$ kind. That is, given Kepler's $T^2 = r^3$, and Huygens' $F = r/T^2$, it follows that the 'F' of gravitation must equal $1/r^2$ (i.e. because $F = r/r^3 = 1/r^2$).

16. Cf. N. R. Hanson, "Leverrier: The Zenith and Nadir of Newtonian Mechanics," *Isis, 53* (1962), 359–78.

Now surely the scientist uses his head in these problem-solving, anomaly-explaining contexts! He reasons! And reasoning has some structure—it moves from stage to stage; this, even before a conclusion is reached and tested. Who would argue that reasoning *only* occurs when one chooses to review the finished argument, that one which terminates finally in a fully tested conclusion? No one should want thus to argue, for it is *obviously* untrue. But those who exclude logical analysis from all stages of research-inquiry save that where the subject matter is the *finished research report*—they are perilously close to being in just such a blameworthy position.

VIII   HD and RD proponents both recognize that their formal criteria for success in argument are precisely the same. In this Peirce was no less acute than Popper. Thus, imagine that one scientist argues from premises A, B, C and an hypothesis H, to a conclusion D (which, although perhaps originally unexpected, is confirmed in fact). Another scientist experimentally encounters the anomalous fact that D, and conjoins this statement with A, B, and C, so as to 'corner' an hypothesis H which, when bracketed with A, B, and C, will possibly 'explain' D.[17] Both scientists have been arguing; both have been using their brains. Differently!

17. This is not a *mere* supposition for the purposes of philosophical exposition. P. A. M. Dirac is an example of a scientist of the first kind, one who succeeded in bracketing many apparently unrelated As, Bs, and Cs of experimental microphysics with the hypothesis H (that electron theory could be applicable even in the regions of relativity-effect energies, and that the fundamental equation for achieving this generality could be of the first order in time, rather than of the second order as with the Klein-Gordon). From all this he unpacked the wholly unexpected conclusion D (that some electrons should, in principle, have a property designated by '–W', which was originally read as 'negative energy', but later became intelligible as 'positive charge').

Carl Anderson, on the other hand, experimentally encountered the anomalous fact that D (that some cosmic rays 'materialized' particles in a cloud chamber—particles which had to be electronic, given their energies and masses—but which curved towards the negative pole in the surrounding magnetic field). After much reflection on this D, Anderson conjoined the statement with the 'orthodox' As, Bs, and Cs of the electron theory of the late 1920s so as ultimately to feel cornered ('by symmetry considerations') with H, the hypothesis opting for the existence of a positively charged electron!

Notes Toward a Logic of Discovery

But the criterion for their having *succeeded* with their different tasks will be just this: *that D follows from A, B, C, and H*. If either the first, or the second, scientist was mistaken in thinking D to be entailed by A, B, C, and H, then his reasoning fails.[18]

However, if the ultimate *logical* criteria for success or failure in either case are the same, then whatever distinguished these two scientific arguments must be nonlogical, and therefore (so the typical HD position develops) must be *merely psychological*. This is the strong form of the thesis that, though the aspects of scientific thinking distinguished by the HD and RD accounts may be interesting to psychologists, they contain nothing of importance for philosophers and logicians. It is the thesis that only psychological considerations distinguish (1′) and (2′) above. My intention is to attack that conclusion—under Peirce's banner, for he never marshaled his arguments specifically for this encounter.

Consider a logic teacher presenting a problem to his class. One orthodox assignment might be this: "Here are three premises: A, B, and C. From these alone generate the theorem D." The teacher is here charging his students to find what follows from premises written 'at the top of the page'. This is related to the traveler's puzzlement when he asks, "Here I am, river to the left, mountains to the right, canyon ahead, blizzard to the rear; *where do I go from here?*"

Contrast this with the quite different assignment a logic teacher might give: "Here is a theorem D. Find *any* three premises, A, B, and C, *from which* D is generable." Here he gives D to his students 'written at the bottom of the page', as it were. He requires them to work back from this to three premises which, if they were written at the top of the page, would be a 'that from which' D follows. Analogously, the traveler's question would be "Would I be able to *return to here* from over there? or over there? or there?"

---

18. The existence of positrons is entailed by the Dirac electron theory—and this *was* the case before this novel particle was first observed. But when Anderson first observed the 'oppositely curving electronic particle' he accounted for it by finding an H from which the new tracks' description followed, to wit, that positrons exist!

These two queries of the traveler will be answered, and appraised, by the same geographical and cartographical criteria—"Is there a route connecting point A, B, C with point D?" Whether one is at A, B, C asking if he can get from there to D, or asking while at D whether he could return from some other point A, B, C back to D—the ultimate geographical issue is only whether some traversable route connects A, B, C and D. The shepherd's answer to the traveler, "You can't get there from here," is not wholly a joke. There are some Ds which cannot be reached from a given A, B, C—and some A, B, Cs are unattainable from a given D.[19]

Similarly, the criteria for assessing the logic students' answers are the same whether the teacher has asked his question in terms of *premiss unpacking,* or in terms of *premiss hunting:* "Is there a logical route connecting A, B, C with D?" Whether one is at D (the bottom of the page) and looking 'up' for some A, B, C, H from which he could get back to D, or whether one begins at A, B, C, H (the top of the page) and asks whether he can make it down to D—that these are different is not relevant in the strictest logic. But that alone doesn't make the difference just a psychological one; I will argue that it is a difference of the deepest conceptual importance. The question of the existence of a route, logical or geographical, may be independent of whether the route is traversed from one end to the other, or from the other end to the one: from A, B, C, H to D, or from D to A, B, C, H. This does not make the direction of travel just a matter for psychologists, however.

It is often supposed that when considering the *form* of an argument one should think of it as if it were 'mathematical'. It is imagined that the ways in which logicians and mathematicians actually argue somehow illuminates the issue of logical form. This is false. Mathematicians—no less than other reasonable men—argue sometimes from premisses to conclusions, and sometimes from an anomaly to its explanation, independently of any abstract

19. E.g. the summit of Mt. Everest just cannot be reached from an advanced camp on the northern face; and in a Piper Cub (J3) one simply cannot get to Aspen, Colorado, from Boulder via Long's Peak.

Notes Toward a Logic of Discovery

questions concerning whether some abstract logical route connects the beginning point of the argument with its terminus. The de facto reasonings of pure mathematicians are just like ours. They have a 'progressive' arrow built into them; they proceed from a starting point to a finish line. Which is which—this will always be a contextual question.[20]

The logical *form* of an argument does not progress at all. It is static, time-independent, problem-neutral; above the battles of natural and formal science alike. Hence, if 'deducing' is what logicians and mathematicians *do* when arguing from premises to conclusions (in contradistinction to 'deductive' qua the abstract *form* of some argument structures) then the word "deduction" cannot, in the same sense, demarcate the formal characteristics of one kind of argument as against others, e.g. inductive, probabilistic, analogical . . . etc. Because even in these latter kinds of argument one often proceeds from premises to conclusions.[21] If deduction is what someone does during some of the de facto business of reasoning, then alternative ways of proceeding with one's inferential reflections might be different, and they might bear different names, e.g., 'hypothetico-deduction', 'retroduction', etc. This may be so even though from a *strictly* formal standpoint nothing can distinguish the procedures—which is just what I'm proposing in this HD versus RD case.

Thus, just as arguing from the top of a page down to a conclusion differs conceptually from working from a conclusion 'up' to premises at the top (even when the logical form of each statement-

---

20. Given a haystack, one may be obliged to seek a needle therein; but, to have *sat* on a needle in a haystack may make one ask "How did that get here?" —a question not just psychologically distinct from the first.

21. Consider the expression 'a false deduction'. This makes no sense when 'deduction' characterizes the absolute and necessary connections between propositions, since if D does not follow from A, B, C it is not a deduction from those premises at all; how odd to call it 'a false deduction' in that case. Whereas if a problem-solver, after reflection, sets out his conclusion as 'D'— then one might very well refer to his inferential activity as constituting 'false deduction', by which it would be meant that he stated as his conclusion from A, B, C a proposition (D) which does not follow. What did he do? He deduced$_1$ that D. Is D a deduction$_2$ from A, B, C? No! Then his was a *false* deduction$_1$!

cluster is identical to that of the other), so also, arguing from initial conditions-plus-hypothesis (A, B, C, H) down to an observation statement (D) is conceptually different from, although logically identical to, working 'up' from an anomaly (D) to some hypothesis (H) which, when conjoined with initial conditions (A, B, C) will entail, and hence may explain, the anomaly.[22] The only question here is, "Does *some* logical route connect A, B, C, H with D?" If none does, then neither a retroduction from D nor a hypothetico-deduction from A, B, C, H will be forthcoming.

The HD account, again, centers on hypothesis testing. It stresses the generating of observation statements, D, from premisses A, B, C, H. When the Ds 'square with the facts'[23] H is 'insofar forth confirmed' (another Peirce-ism). The typical exposition gives A, B, C, as known, H as conjectured, while D_1, D_2, D_3 . . . have yet to be 'unpacked' from this premiss cluster.[24]

---

22. The contrast between 'entailing D' and 'explaining D' is quite intentional —and quite contrary to the Hempel-Oppenheim account of explanation (at least in some of its versions). That 'all αs are βs' does not explain why this α is a β—although it does entail that this α is a β. H, to 'explain' D, therefore, must be the right 'kind' of hypothesis—about which more later.

23. As *Patterns of Discovery*, Chapters 1 and 2, will indicate, I am cognizant of the intricate complexities lurking within the illusory simplicity of this expression 'square with the facts'. However, the *ad rem* is different here, and we'll resist all temptation to discuss the labyrinthine logic of 'facts'.

24. The analogy between what the mathematician does during *some* of his problem solving and what the scientist is taken to do always (by the HD philosopher) is again instructive. The scientist does not know in advance *what* observation statements D_1, D_2, D_3 will be generable from A, B, C, H. This is what makes this HD procedure an indirect test of H (after the latter has been formulated, conjoined with A, B, C, and set into a theoretical framework of 'auxiliary hypotheses'). In both mathematics and natural science, arguments often exfoliate deductively[1] ; they proceed from 'the top of the page' down to the D-statements. *This* does not identify the two disciplines, however. The formal scientist is not concerned with the empirical truth of A, B, C, or H, nor with that of the conclusions drawable therefrom. That a conclusion D (whether factually true *or* false) is validly generable from premisses A, B, C, H (again, true or false doesn't matter), this will be his one concern. A natural scientist proceeding in the HD manner, however, will begin with initial conditions A, B,

Notes Toward a Logic of Discovery

When wearing his RD cap, the scientist begins his inquiry in puzzlement—indeed, quite often in astonishment. This is the 'normal' context of discovery. After unpacking a well-established theory, replete with Hs, into the expected Ds, the scientist discovers that nature is not described by some of these latter. His expectations (and those of the theory) are thus thwarted. Hence he is puzzled, perplexed, confused, but these psychological epithets should not becloud the conceptual structure of that which may yet resolve his consternation. He has no reason to doubt A, B, C; their independent verification is what made them initial conditions. His astonishment consists in noting that the apparently orthodox H does not, when conjoined with A, B, C, generate descriptions of the facts.

Thus the question: 'Given the anomaly D, and initial conditions A, B, C—from the hypothesis H′ (i.e. any one other than the orthodox H) does D follow when H′ is bracketed with A, B and C?'

C established *as true;* their factual truth is what makes them conditions. The truth status of H, of course, remains unknown; all that is clear about H is that, if factually true, it *could* 'explain' D. After D is deduced from this set and disclosed to describe the facts, H may be said to have become 'probabilified'. The natural scientist's concern is to determine whether a given H can thus be raised to the same degree of acceptability as distinguish the initial conditions A, B, C. This he settles by enlarging and diversifying the set of observation statements D_1, D_2, D_3 ... the regular confirmation of which will systematically raise H's probability. This, then, demarcates sharply the epistemic context within which the mathematician and natural scientist work. Still, vis-à-vis the *direction* of argument there is no demarcation to be made; the mathematician *and* the scientist will both (on occasion) argue from the top of the page down. This is traditionally described as 'deducing$_1$'. Often the thrust of Holmes' comment, "Simple deduction, my dear Watson," is to the effect that the reasoning in question has proceeded from the previously accepted to what should be expected. But just as often the mathematician and the scientist will argue from the bottom of the page 'up'. This is one of the things Peirce identifies as 'retroducing'. It proceeds from an unexpected (but indubitably encountered) anomaly, to a premiss cluster most parts of which are already accepted. One part of it may be quite novel, however—as both Aristotle and Whewell undertook to stress.

Consider these two schemata:

HD CHARACTERIZATION	RD CHARACTERIZATION

$$A, B, C + H \qquad\qquad D_1\ D_2\ D_3 \ldots$$

initial conditions plus hypoth-   anomalies, incompatible with
esis   HD 'unpacking' of orthodox
                                    Hs

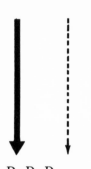 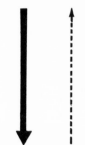

$$D_1\ D_2\ D_3 \ldots \qquad A, B, C + H_1\ or\ H_2\ or\ H_3\ or$$

observation statements—as yet   established conditions of in-
untested in some cases   quiry plus possible explana-
                                  tory hypotheses

The solid arrows represent the actual order of the scientist's argument—the way in which he does, in fact, wend his way from the beginning to the end of his problem. The actual beginning in the HD case is at A, B, C + H, which set is then unpacked into the possibly heretofore unformulated D_1, D_2, D_3. In the other case (RD), the occasion for inquiry is the anomaly D, or the anomaly-set D_{1-3}. The rational moves from there are toward a premiss cluster A, B, C plus some H which can 'explain' the anomaly.[25] *The dotted arrows, however, represent the logical*

25. That is, explain the anomaly by 'engulfing it within the conceptually familiar', or at least within the 'intelligible-in-principle'. As noted earlier, a mere statistical generalization about all Ds may entail some given D, but may fail to engulf it within the familiar [the intelligible], the comprehensible—and hence it will not constitute an explanation, however deductively fertile a generalization it may be.

order of the progressions. In both characterizations the dotted arrows have the same sense—'they point the same way in logical space', towards the particulars, D_1, D_2, D_3. Hence the logical criteria for appraising the validity of arguments in either form are identical.

Here, then, are two argument-schemata which, vis-à-vis logical structure, are one and the same. But, vis-à-vis their de facto conceptual development within the problem-solving context, they are clearly different—and not merely psychologically so! The HD one 'starts from' initial conditions plus hypothesis and terminates in low-level, observationally testable claims. The other (RD) 'begins with' statements of actual observations—perhaps unexpected in HD terms (and hence 'anomalous')—and terminates in a statement of initial conditions A, B, C, and some perhaps heretofore unformulated hypothesis H.

Consider once again the claim that this difference can be no more than psychological since both the arguments are structured identically; they are built on but one logical scheme. This claim cannot be correct. My reason for saying this is that the same conceptual probe leads to quite different reactions in the two cases.

That probe consists in this: that from consistent premises, A, B, C, H, *any* two resulting theorems (e.g. D_1 and D_2) *must* themselves be consistent. Whereas, given any two sets of premises—A, B, C, H as against A', B', C', H'—either of which may resolve some anomaly D, it is not the case that these need be mutually consistent.

Thus consider the premiss-set—A, B, C *and* 'John is a bachelor.' If these four premises are consistent, then everything (D_1–D_n) that follows from them must also be mutually consistent—e.g., 'John is unmarried', 'John is male', 'John is an adult', etc. But begin instead from the low-level claim D: 'John is male'. This can be shown to follow from A, B, C *and* 'John is a bachelor'. But it also follows from A, B, C *and* 'John is a married uncle'. These two premiss-sets, however, although each entails D, are certainly not consistent with each other. And since conceptually different answers result from this single probe, the two characterizations must therefore be conceptually different and not merely psychologically so. It's not just a matter of impressions, or 'how one feels'.

IX   Here it might well be objected: "Yes, 'John is a bachelor' and 'John is a married uncle' *are* inconsistent, but *not* with respect to just what is required in order to generate the single conclusion 'John is male'. Concerning *that* conclusion, being married or unmarried is irrelevant; 'being a bachelor' and 'being an uncle' do the premissory work—and these are quite consistent. Indeed, this must be so by the principle

$$\{ (p \dashv q) \cdot \Diamond \sim q \} \dashv \sim (\sim p \dashv q)$$

['If p entails q when q is not necessary, then not p does not also entail q'].''
     "The only acceptable analysis," the objector continues, "must be this: that when

$$(r \cdot p) \cdot (p \dashv q) \qquad then \ q$$

and also

$$(\sim r \cdot p) \cdot (p \dashv q) \qquad then \ q.$$

Hence a single anomalous observation statement (q here, which corresponds to our Ds earlier), can follow from two mutually incompatible premiss-sets only when the specific incompatibility plays no immediate role in the deduction."
     This objection is potent. But it does not really touch the conceptual issue. It remains the case, just as before the objection arose, that any A, B, C, H, R—if consistent—will entail only compatible conclusions $D_1, D_2, D_3 \ldots$ etc. But an anomaly (D_4) might be 'explained' not only by different, independent, nonoverlapping and compatible premiss-sets—e.g. by A, B, C, H, R as

against M, N, L, O, P—but also by *incompatible* premiss-sets—
e.g. by A, B, C, H, R as against A, B, C, H, $\sim$R. The R and the
$\sim$R (as with 'bachelor' and 'married uncle') may be, admittedly,
redundant and uninvolved in this particular and local derivation
of D_4. But redundant or not, the conceptual distinction preserves
itself in fact, and rules out the 'mere psychology' interpretation.
All conclusion-sets derivable from consistent premisses are themselves compatible. But not all premiss-sets from which a given
conclusion-set is derivable will themselves be compatible. This
way of putting the matter marks a genuine conceptual difference
despite the fact that any given RD argument may have a logically
identical HD analogue. The difference in the direction and intention of the two schemata stakes out different ranges of conceptual
development possible to RD and HD argumentation.[26]

Moreover, in characterizing premiss-sets as they are imbedded
in *scientific theories*, no premisses are ever *wholly* redundant in
the degenerate logical sense seen above. For, although R and $\sim$R
may be redundant for this one accounting for D_4, they will not be
redundant in general—as would be a tautology—not in the total
undertaking of distinguishing the whole theories within which
these arguments occur. Thus, in the undulatory theory of light,
R might have signified that a light ray *decelerates* on entering a
denser medium, whereas in the particle theory, $\sim$R might have
had it that light *accelerates* on entering a denser medium. Neither
this R nor this $\sim$R would have been required immediately in the
derivation of D_4, e.g. that the sines of the angles of incidence and
refraction stand in a certain ratio to each other, this ratio being
a function of the media at hand. Still, *explaining* this latter phenomenon will involve reference ultimately not just to the premiss-
set A, B, C, H,—which may be identical in both the wave theory
and in the particle theory. The explanations will, sooner or later,
involve A, B, C, H, R, in the one case, and A, B, C, H, $\sim$R, in
the other, where R and $\sim$R may have concerned the ultimate

26. In general, when philosopher X 'scores' a genuine logical point against
philosopher Y, it does not help Y to paint the point as 'redundant', 'trivial' or
'insignificant'. Only the detection of a *logical* invalidity can aid Y in his rebuttal.
Besides, 'redundant' is not a psychological epithet at all.

'fine structure' of electromagnetic radiation. So the conceptual difference between RD and HD argumentations remains (despite the identity of their ex post facto logical reconstructions), and the difference is not really trivialized by the 'redundancy' move of our objector; triviality is determinable only when considering the totality of a scientific theory, not simply local and specific inferences.

X   Sounding our 'RD theme' within the three-part Fugue called 'A Logic of Discovery' has largely determined the shape and structure of the other two lines in Peirce's Prelude. For clearly, given that an RD resolution of the fact of some anomaly, D_4—given that this resolution will consist only in the identification of an H_1, and H_2, and H_3 . . . or an H_n, any one of which *could* explain the anomaly—given this it seems clear that retroductive inference terminates *not* in the advancing of a single, specific, and detailed H, but rather in the delineation of what *type* of H is most plausibly to be considered as worthy of further serious attention. It is this determination which makes it clear that H_1, H_2, H_3 . . . or H_n *could* explain D_4; they are all hypotheses of the right type.[27]

Thus a shocking anomaly becomes somewhat less disturbing when one has puzzled out what *kind* of hypothesis could explain it. This 'puzzling out', we are clearly instructed by the history of science, usually moves on RD rails which, although they may finally lead to any one of a very large number of specific explanatory hypotheses, will at least be heading in a direction. (This is the point of Peirce's words in 5.188.)

The decision concerning what *kind* of H is the most plausible to entertain is itself dependent on larger considerations. It is the structure of our presently established scientific theories, and the 'shape' of our most reliable conceptual frameworks, that highlight H-types for the problem solver. Much as it is only against the background of 'the intelligible' and 'the conceptually compre-

27. Thus the *color* of the spheres in Galileo's inclined plane demonstration did not plausibly seem to be a determinant of the ball's velocity at any given instant, nor did the dispositions of Jupiter's moons, nor did the number of bird chirps audible at that time; these would all have been deemed hypotheses of the wrong type, and with good reason.

Notes Toward a Logic of Discovery

hensible' that anomalies stand out at all, so also it is in these same terms that the scientist comes to know which types of H will do the job, and which types will not.

Concerning the 'fit' of concepts into larger theoretical frameworks, my book *Patterns of Discovery* is devoted to the discussion of this. Hence there is little need to pursue that ambitious subject of inquiry further here. It is enough to have perceived, even if dimly, a denotatum for the title 'A Logic of Discovery'—and to have suggested a way of composing into one single improvisation the three themes that Peirce has developed under this title.

Thus a philosophically respectable 'Logic of Discovery' would be

(1) an area for inquiry, not a manual of conclusions;

(2) a concern with scientific problem solving and its conceptual characteristics, not a logical reconstruction of 'finished research reports';

(3) a study of the inferential moves from the recognition of anomalies, to

(4) the determination of which *types* of hypothesis might serve to 'explain' those anomalies, where

(5) 'explain' means the fitting of jarring, surprising anomalies into intelligible patterns of ideas, comprehensible frameworks of accepted scientific theories.

In short, Peirce's 'Notes Toward a Logic of Discovery'—marshaled as above—would locate an important area of philosophical inquiry which is not taken seriously enough by philosophers today. It would deny that such an inquiry was fundamentally psychological in its interest, just as it would deny that it has anything to do with the composition of 'discovery manuals'. It would be an analytical examination of what is, and has been, good reasoning in support of H's being the *kind* of hypothesis that might well explain some perplexity. After all, thinking one's way out of a labyrinth is every bit as challenging and worthy a philosophical datum as is surveying the shortest route out (as through a rearview mirror) once one has left the labyrinth.

Chapter 3   Action, Conduct, and Self-Control

Richard J. Bernstein

When philosophers of the future turn their attention to writing the history of philosophy during our time, my hunch is that two concepts will emerge as dominant: perception and action. One of the most striking features of the contemporary scene—even among philosophic movements where there has been little or no dialogue, such as the continental phenomenological tradition and the movement of linguistic analysis that has been so influential in the English-speaking world—has been the preoccupation with the cluster of issues surrounding the concepts of perception and action. The similarities of these two movements go deeper than a common concern with these issues. Although the idiom is different, the insight is frequently shared. In both movements there has been an antidualistic or more generally an anti-Cartesian bias. Since Cartesianism has set the framework for most modern philosophy, these movements can be viewed as rebellions against the mainstream of modern philosophy. Both have tried to show us how much more there is to perception and action than exists in the limited world of traditional empiricists and rationalists; both have provided fresh perspectives that break away from the rigid dichotomies of mind *and* body, thought *and* language, subject *and* object, and especially thought *and* action. Whether we focus on the Wittgensteinian concept of a "form of life" or the phenomenological concept of a *Lebenswelt*, we discover a new orientation for reappraising old problems.

We are also coming to realize how close Peirce's outlook is to the temper and approach of contemporary philosophic investigations. Contemporary philosophy, in many of its diverse forms, is

66

Action, Conduct, and Self-Control

pervaded by a Peircean spirit, although it would be misleading to claim that this is a direct consequence of his influence. It is Peirce who proclaimed, "The elements of every concept enter into logical thought at the gate of perception and make their exit at the gate of purposive action; and whatever cannot show its passports at both those two gates is to be arrested as unauthorized by reason" (5.212). In this essay, I plan to focus on Peirce's analysis of action and the related notions of conduct and self-control, for I believe that we find here some of his most profound insights as well as some of his most notable failures. By exploring these concepts and the ways in which they connect with other key ideas, we can appreciate the thrust of his philosophy, and also show the basis for a fruitful dialogue between Peirce and more recent investigations of these issues.[1] But first, as Locke phrased it, we must help "in clearing the ground a little and removing some of the rubbish that lies in the way of knowledge."

Bertrand Russell once accused pragmatism—the movement that Peirce founded—of glorifying the American love of action and being little more than an expression of American commercialism. However wrongheaded this view is, and it is refuted on almost every page of Peirce, James, and Dewey, it is still the picture that comes to mind when "pragmatism" is mentioned. John Dewey put Russell in his place when he said that this suggestion is "of that order of interpretation which would say that English neo-realism is a reflection of the aristocratic snobbery of the English; the tendency of French thought to dualism an expression of an alleged Gallic disposition to keep a mistress in addition to a wife; and the idealism of Germany a manifestation of an ability to elevate beer and sausage into a higher synthesis with the spiritual values of Beethoven and Wagner."[2] The same general type of criticism was familiar to Peirce. In one of his late papers he set forth the fundamentals of his "pragmaticism" (a name—"which

1. For a discussion of the concept of perception that complements this analysis of action, see my article, "Peirce's Theory of Perception," *Studies in the Philosophy of Charles Sanders Peirce*, ed. Edward C. Moore and Richard Robin, pp. 165–89.

2. John Dewey, *Characters and Events* (2 vols. New York, 1929), 2, 543.

is ugly enough to be safe from kidnappers" [5.414]—he used to designate his own distinctive variety of pragmatism). The Questioner in this dialogue asks in exasperation, "Well, if you choose so to make Doing the Be-all and the End-all of human life, why do you not make meaning to consist simply in doing?" Peirce squarely answers, "Forcibly put! . . . It must be admitted . . . that if pragmaticism really made Doing to be the Be-all and the End-all of life, that would be its death. For to say that we live for the mere sake of action, as action, would be to say that there is no such thing as rational purport" (5.429). But while it is easy to say what is *not* Peirce's view of action, it is much more difficult to discover what precisely is the role of action, and what is the aim of human life. To get clearer about the issues with which Peirce was struggling, we need to gain some perspective on the philosophic climate in which Peirce was working.

The specter that haunts most of philosophy in the latter part of the nineteenth century is that of Hegel. Although Peirce did not come to philosophy through the study of Hegel, as Dewey did, he recognized close affinities between pragmaticism and Hegelianism. At the same time Peirce insisted that Hegel had left something out that pragmaticism added to our understanding of man in the universe, something that drastically transformed the import of Hegelianism. What Peirce thought that Hegel had neglected is the same thing that Kierkegaard and Marx, in different and independent ways, had also pointed out. All three accused Hegel of failing to appreciate the concrete meaning and role of human action. Whether or not this charge against Hegel is accurate— recent Hegelian scholarship has challenged its legitimacy—it nevertheless defined the philosophic stance of Peirce, Kierkegaard, and Marx and thus affected pragmatism, existentialism, and Marxism.

The issue is dramatically epitomized in Marx's famous eleventh thesis on Feuerbach, "The philosophers have only *interpreted* the world, in various ways: the point, however, is to *change* it." Marx wrote this when he was in his twenties and the concept of action or *praxis* became the core of his philosophic-empirical outlook. *Praxis* as the central category of Marxism passed into oblivion in

Action, Conduct, and Self-Control

many orthodox interpretations of Marx, but it is once again prominent in the current revival of Marxism, especially in the most recent work of Sartre. Action, for Marx, is basically a social category. In Kierkegaard, the dissatisfaction with Hegel and the system builders takes the form of emphasizing the distinctive existential status of individual action. In a variety of ways, Kierkegaard shows us how the uniqueness of human existence, decision, and action eludes the essentialist categories of Hegel and, more generally, those of most Western philosophy. Peirce's complaint against Hegel is metaphorically represented when he tells us, "The capital error of Hegel which permeates his whole system in every part of it is that he almost altogether ignores the Outward Clash" (8.41). We shall soon see how this complaint is related to Peirce's view of action. Or again Peirce says:

> The truth is that pragmaticism is closely allied to the Hegelian absolute idealism, from which, however, it is sundered by its vigorous denial that the third category (which Hegel degrades to a mere stage of thinking) suffices to make the world, or is even so much as self-sufficient. Had Hegel, instead of regarding the first two stages with his smile of contempt, held on to them as independent or distinct elements of the triune Reality, pragmaticists might have looked up to him as the great vindicator of their truth (5.436).

What is this "Outward Clash," and what are the "distinct elements of the triune Reality"? Peirce is alluding to his categorial scheme of Firstness, Secondness, and Thirdness, the ultimate categories of experience, reality, and being. By sketching the use that Peirce makes of these categories, especially in the analysis of experience, we can provide the necessary orientation for appreciating his contribution to our understanding of action, conduct, and self-control.

I   Writing to Lady Welby in 1904, Peirce tells us "I was long ago (1867) led, after only three or four years' study, to throw all ideas into the three classes of Firstness, of Secondness, and of Thirdness. This sort of notion is as distasteful to me as to anybody; and for years, I endeavored to pooh-pooh and refute it; but it long ago conquered me completely. Disagreeable as it is to attribute such meaning to numbers, and to a triad above all, it is true as it is disagreeable" (8.328). Peirce used this categorial scheme in multifarious and sometimes inconsistent ways, but throughout his writings he maintains that these categories designate elements ingredient in all experience, reality, and being; that these categories are irreducible in the sense that we cannot adequately account for the aspects of phenomena that each category singles out by exclusive reference to some combination of the other categories, and that we need no further categories to give a comprehensive, coherent account of experience, reality, and being. Peirce did think that he could "prove" the necessity and irreducibility of the categories, but it is never quite clear what he has "proven" (see 5.469; 1.345; 5.82 ff.). He certainly fails to demonstrate that the categories are necessary, sufficient, and irreducible in all the uses that he makes of them. I do not think that this is a serious failure of his philosophy. On the contrary, it helps us to see how the categorial scheme actually functions. The dominant spirit of Peirce's meaning is reflected in the passage cited from the letter to Lady Welby. There is a descriptive, empirical, pragmatic temper manifested in Peirce's use of the categories.[3] The "proof," or more accurately the adequacy of the categorial scheme, is to be found in the ways in which Peirce uses it to illuminate fundamental similarities and differences in everything we encounter.

It is in phenomenology or what Peirce calls "phaneroscopy" that he makes the most suggestive and detailed use of the categories. "Phaneroscopy is the description of the *phaneron;* and by the phaneron I mean the collective total of all that is in any way or in any sense present to the mind, quite regardless of whether it corresponds to any real thing or not" (1.284). Phenomenology or

> *phaneroscopy* is that study which, supported by the direct observation of phanerons and generalizing its observations, signalizes several very broad classes of phanerons; describes

3. Richard Rorty has made a similar point in another context. See his "Pragmatism, Categories, and Language," *Philosophical Review, 60* (1961), 199 ff.

the features of each; shows that although they are so inextricably mixed together that no one can be isolated, yet it is manifest that their characters are quite disparate; then proves, beyond question, that a certain very short list comprises all of these broadest categories of phanerons there are; and finally proceeds to the laborious and difficult task of enumerating the principal subdivisions of those categories (1.286).

Firstness is characterized as "the unanalyzed total impression made by any manifold not thought of as actual fact, but simply as a quality, as simple positive possibility of appearance" (8.329). Firstness is that which is qualitative and immediate; "quality is the monadic element of the world" (1.426). Qualities per se are neither subjective nor objective. Consider the following examples that Peirce offers as illustrations of Firstness or immediate quality: "the scarlet of your royal liveries, the quality itself, independently of its being perceived or remembered" (8.329); "the quality of the emotion upon contemplating a fine mathematical demonstration, the quality of feeling of love" (1.304); "a vague, unobjectified, still less unsubjectified, sense of redness, or of salt taste, or of an ache, or of grief or joy, or of a prolonged musical note" (1.303). We can easily mistake Peirce's point if we think of these qualities as subjective feelings that are somehow locked up in the privacy of our minds. Everything has its distinctive quality. "The tragedy of King Lear has its Firstness, its flavor *sui generis*" (1.531). The poetic mood comes closest to that state in which we are most directly aware of qualitative immediacy. (Cf. 5.44.)

What is Peirce "up to" in calling attention to this myriad variety of qualities and dubbing them all "Firstness"? What is the point of his claim that this is an irreducible aspect of all experience? First, it should be noted how Peirce departs from traditional discussions of quality. In a good deal of traditional philosophy, the quality or the "whatness" of something has been thought of as a basic epistemological unit, as the primary object of knowledge. But what Peirce means by quality is something that is precognitive, something that is *felt* or *had*. We, of course, know that we are aware of qualities, but this "knowledge that" is not to be confused with the actual awareness or direct experience of qualities. Secondly, Peirce includes far more under the category of Firstness than is to be found in the standard classification of primary and secondary qualities. There are unique, pervasive, ineffable qualities such as the quality of fear or the quality of *King Lear*. Peirce's exploration of the diversity of qualities and his claim that this is an aspect of every experience can be viewed as an attempt to give proper due to a feature of experience that had been neglected in the tradition of Western philosophy. In this respect, Peirce is a representative of many late nineteenth- and early twentieth-century philosophers, including Bergson, James, Dewey, and Whitehead, who reacted against the "intellectualistic" temper of Western philosophy. All of these philosophers emphasized the concreteness and qualitative immediacy of experience. But unlike Bergson, for example, Peirce did not claim that the direct awareness of qualitative immediacy provides us with direct, intuitive, infallible *knowledge* of reality itself. All knowledge, according to Peirce, involves Thirdness and is essentially fallible.

Immediate quality or Firstness is mere unattached possibility. We never really encounter qualities as mere possibilities, but only qualities embodied in some concrete form. The element of quality is abstracted or prescinded from the complex total experience; it is not something distinct and separable from the rest of experience. This brings us to Peirce's category of Secondness. It is under this category that action (as distinct from conduct) falls. The phenomenological manifestation of Secondness is to be found in "the sense of shock," surprise, struggle, or wherever there is "as much a sense of resisting as of being acted upon" (5.45). By "struggle" Peirce means "mutual action between two things regardless of any sort of third or medium, and in particular regardless of any law of action" (1.322). Secondness is essentially dual; indeed this is the basis for distinguishing this category from the monadic simplicity of Firstness. But when Secondness is used to focus our attention on an irreducible feature of experience, it signifies that *"not mere twoness but active oppugnancy is in it"* (8.291).

You get this kind of consciousness in some approach to purity when you put your shoulder against a door and try to force it open. You have a sense of resistance and at the same time a sense of effort. There can be no resistance without effort; there can be no effort without resistance. They are only two ways of describing the same experience. It is a double consciousness. We become aware of ourself by becoming aware of the not-self. The waking state is a consciousness of reaction; and as the consciousness *itself* is two-sided, so it has also two varieties; namely, action, where our modification of other things is more prominent than their reaction on us, and perception, where their effect on us is overwhelmingly greater than our effect on them. . . . The idea of other, of *not*, becomes a very pivot of thought. To this element I give the name of Secondness (1.324).

Peirce's extremely fertile imagination is at work. We see that his use of the categories highlights basic similarities which have frequently been ignored. For Secondness is prominent in both the notions of experience and existence. "It is the compulsion, the absolute constraint upon us to think otherwise than we have been thinking that constitutes experience" (1.336). "Experience is that determination of belief and cognition generally which the course of life has forced upon a man. One may lie about it; but one cannot escape the fact that some things *are* forced upon his cognition. There is the element of brute force, existing whether you opine it exists or not" (2.138). As for existence, Peirce tells us that *"existence* means reaction with the environment, and so is a dynamic character" (5.503). "The *existent* is that which reacts against other things" (8.191).

Once again we may feel uneasy about this imaginative grouping of phenomena and concepts as manifesting Secondness. But consider the suggestiveness of this classification. For example, we can view Peirce's claim that Secondness is the dominant characteristic of experience from the perspective of the entire tradition of empiricism. The essential insight of this tradition is that all ideas and hypotheses must ultimately be brought to the test of experience. But why is experience the touchstone for testing all knowledge claims? This is because of the brute compulsion of experience itself. "Experience" refers "to that which is forced upon a man's recognition, will-he nill-he" (5.613). There is a deep irony in the development of the empiricist tradition. The original insight of the essential compulsive ingredient in experience that is so prominent in Locke's philosophy was eventually betrayed, as empiricism became more subjectivistic and phenomenalistic. What seemed so clear to Locke and was the starting point of his philosophy, viz., that our observation of external sensible objects and of the internal operations of the mind "are the fountains of knowledge, from whence all the ideas we have, or can naturally have, do spring"[4] became more and more problematic as empiricism became more skeptical. Indeed, the existence of the external world became one of the nagging problems of empiricism. From Peirce's point of view, we can say that the subjectivistic and phenomenalistic varieties of empiricism smothered the original insight that experience is irreducibly compulsive and dyadic, that it exhibits Secondness.

We can also appreciate the significance of Peirce's use of the category of Secondness from an entirely different orientation. Peirce is calling our attention to the "over againstness" in all experience and existence that has been a key emphasis in the existentialist tradition. The internal oppositional tension of human existence is the basis for Kierkegaard's claim that human existence is never completely "overcome," or to use the Hegelian term, *aufgehoben*. When the existentialists speak of the bruteness of human existence and its resistance to being taken up in a system of thought, when they insist on the inescapable facticity of human life, they are emphasizing what Peirce calls Secondness. The existentialists have also claimed that the "waking state is a consciousness of reaction" (Peirce, quoted above); and the statement that "the idea of other, of *not,* becomes a very pivot of thought" might well have appeared in Sartre's *Being and Nothing.*

4. John Locke, *An Essay Concerning Human Understanding,* ed. A. C. Fraser (2 vols. Oxford, 1894), *1,* 122.

Action, Conduct, and Self-Control

Peirce's use of the categories shows us a revealing way of linking up existentialism with a tradition that many have thought to be alien to the spirit of existentialism—empiricism.

The linking of different philosophic traditions is directly related to the finer analysis of perception and action. Peirce shows how perception and action are intimately related. There is no perception without action and no action without perception. The exploration of the intimate dependence of these two concepts is central to both recent analytic and phenomenological investigations. The claim of Stuart Hampshire, which might be taken as a manifesto of this new approach, is in the direct tradition of Peirce.

> The deepest mistake in empiricist theories of perception, descending from Berkeley and Hume, has been the representation of human beings as passive observers receiving impressions from 'outside' of the mind, where the 'outside' includes their own bodies. In fact I find myself from the beginning able to act upon objects around me. In this context to act is to move at will my own body, that persisting physical thing, and thereby to bring about perceived movements of other physical things. I not only perceive my body, I also control it; I not only perceive external objects, I also manipulate them.[5]

The final category, Thirdness, is at once the most intriguing and difficult one to understand. Habits, laws, rules, potentiality, intentions, concepts, signs, meaning, and conduct are all classified as Thirds. Peirce's favorite example of a triadic relation is "giving." "A *gives* B to C. This does not consist of A's throwing B away and its accidentally hitting C. . . . If that were all, it would not be a genuine triadic relation, but merely one dyadic relation followed by another. There need be no motion of the thing given. Giving is a transfer of the right of property. Now right is a matter of law, and law is a matter of thought and meaning" (1.345). We cannot give an adequate account of the relation of giving by describing it in terms of physical (or even mental) juxtaposition.

5. Stuart Hampshire, *Thought and Action* (London, 1959), p. 47.

What is distinctive about giving is that there are some conventions, rules, or customs by virtue of which an act is giving and not just physical displacement. These conventions, rules, or customs are essential constituents of the type of action or conduct that is properly designated "giving." Giving is a form of conduct. Consider the closely related example of A's making a contract with C. "To say that A signs the document D and C signs the document D, no matter what the contents of that document, does not make a contract. The contract lies in the intent. And what is the intent? It is that certain conditional rules shall govern the conduct of A and of C" (1.475). Peirce, in his analysis of Thirdness, foreshadows discussions of rules that have played such a prominent role in recent analytic philosophy. An adequate account of experience and, more generally, reality, demands a recognition of the pervasiveness of rulelikeness or lawlikeness.

Just as there is an element of qualitative immediacy and brute opposition in all experience, so too there is an element of conditional generality or lawlikeness that "goes beyond anything that can ever be done or have happened. . . . No matter how far specification has gone, it can be carried further; and the general condition covers all that incompletable possibility" (1.475). There is a future-oriented dimension, an openness or essential indeterminacy characteristic of all manifestations of Thirdness. In the language of the categories, we can say that although Thirdness requires Secondness (and Secondness requires Firstness), Thirdness cannot be reduced to Secondness or Firstness. No appeal to an aggregate of Seconds can be sufficient to yield a Third. Or to make the point more concrete and relevant to our specific concern, there is no conduct without action, but action (insofar as we consider it to be brute action or as exhibiting the intrinsic duality of Secondness) is not sufficient to yield the conditional generality of conduct.

II   Thus far we may have a "feel" for what Peirce is saying, but it is not yet clear why he claims what he does and what is the philosophic significance of these claims. The import of the categorial scheme will become clearer as we explore the distinction between action and conduct.

Action, Conduct, and Self-Control

Action is perfectly determinate: there is no indeterminateness or vagueness in brute action. It happens once and for all; it is irrational or, more neutrally, nonrational. Action insofar as it approximates pure Secondness is singular and antigeneral; it exhibits what Duns Scotus called *hic et nunc*. I have spoken of action insofar as it approximates pure Secondness, because we must keep in mind that elements distinguished by all three categories are manifested in every experience. There is no such thing as an experience of pure brute action or Secondness, but there is an element of bruteness that can be prescinded or abstracted in the analysis of experience. "There is nothing at all that is absolutely confrontitial; although it is quite true that the confrontitial is continually flowing in upon us" (7.653).

Conduct, as distinguished from brute action, is essentially general. While brute action is singular, conduct is a type or kind of activity. Conduct is closely related to Peirce's central notion of habit. "[Readiness] to act in a certain way under given circumstances and when actuated by a given motive is a habit; and a deliberate, or self-controlled, habit is precisely a belief" (5.480). Though Peirce speaks of habit here in a context in which it is appropriate to speak of "motive" and "control," the notion of habit plays a much broader role in Peirce's philosophy. He argues that everything, whether animate or inanimate, manifests habits. While the use of the term "habit" when applied to entities that are not animate may strike us as excessively anthropomorphic, Peirce is making an extremely important point. The claim that everything manifests habits—"What we call a Thing is a cluster or habit of reactions" (4.157)—is a way of calling attention to the fact that everything in the universe is governed by or exhibits laws, and that these laws are to be understood in terms of the conditional generality characteristic of Thirdness.[6]

Conduct or habit consists of what Peirce calls "would-be's." To say that a person or a thing has a habit means that it *"would* behave (or usually behave) in a certain way *whenever* a certain occasion should arise" (8.380). Although conduct, habits, or

---

6. Cf. Rorty, p. 211, n.

"would-be's" issue in action, "no agglomeration of actual happenings can ever completely fill up the meaning of a 'would-be'"
(5.467). We can now see more clearly why Peirce insists that all
Thirds are future-oriented. While the past is the "storehouse of
knowledge" and "whenever we set out to do anything, we 'go
upon', we base our conduct on facts already known" (5.460); the
laws, habits, and conduct that we come to know are not exhausted
by past regularities. If they were, they would be mere regularities,
not genuine laws or Thirds. The conditional generality of Thirdness is not exhausted by any finite set of past, present, or future
happenings. Furthermore "future facts are the only facts that we
can, in a measure, control; and whatever there may be in the
Future that is not amenable to control are the things that we *shall*
be able to infer, or *should* be able to infer under favorable circumstances" (5.461). When Peirce adds that thinking itself is a kind of
activity or conduct (8.191), that intelligence consists of "acting in a
certain way" (6.286), and that "all thought . . . must necessarily be
in signs" (5.251), many of his most important and provocative
theses fit together into a comprehensive, coherent outlook.

The Pragmatic Maxim itself is primarily concerned with conduct, deliberate conduct, not with actions as discrete happenings.
In its original form Peirce stated the maxim as follows: "Consider
what effects, which might conceivably have practical bearings, we
conceive the object of our conception to have. Then, our conception of these effects is the whole of our conception of the object"
(5.402). At a later date, commenting on what appears to be a
clumsy formation, he pointed out that the

> employment five times over of derivates of *concipere* must
> then have had a purpose. In point of fact it had two. One was
> to show that I was speaking of meaning in no other sense
> than that of *intellectual purport*. The other was to avoid all
> danger of being understood as attempting to explain a con-
> cept by percepts, images, schemata, or anything but concepts.
> I did not, therefore, mean to say that acts, which are more
> strictly singular than anything, could constitute the purport,
> or adequate proper interpretation, of any symbol. . . . Prag-

maticism makes thinking to consist in the living inferential metaboly of symbols whose purport lies in conditional general resolutions to act (5.402, n. 3).

Peirce ultimately identifies the intellectual purport or meaning of a proposition with habits and conduct; the Pragmatic Maxim is intended to single out from "the myriads of forms into which a proposition may be translated . . . that form in which the proposition becomes applicable to human conduct" (5.427). The intellectual purport or meaning is identified with habits and conduct, and these are essentially general and conditional. These are the features that distinguish Peirce's pragmaticism from more common varieties of pragmatism and positivism. What we might call "vulgar" pragmatism and positivism has (unsuccessfully) sought to identify the meaning of propositions with some determinate set of singular consequences or observations. The issue can be put in another way. Most varieties of twentieth-century pragmatism, positivism, and phenomenalism have been nominalistically oriented, i.e. they have assumed or argued that the real entities are only individuals or particulars. Peirce called himself a Scotistic realist and claimed that pragmaticism and the doctrine of realism mutually entail each other. (Cf. 5.453, 5.470, 5.503.) We cannot explore in depth what Peirce means by realism and how he distinguished his doctrine from Platonism. (Cf. 5.470; 8.10, 8.18, 8.30.) The cash value of Peirce's realism is that Thirdness—which is conditional and general, whether manifested in habits, conduct or signs—is irreducible and inescapable. The meaning or intellectual purport that is the primary concern of the pragmaticist consists of habits and conduct; these are the generals or universals that are the inescapable aspects of reality and experience.

III   We can now penetrate further to the heart of Peirce's philosophy, especially to his attempt to show the continuity of thought and action. In our discussion of conduct, we have begun to see the importance of controlled conduct. There are aspects of experience that are beyond or below the level of control. The shock or surprise of experience is something over which we have no control. "The 'hardness' of fact lies in the insistency of the percept, its entirely irrational insistency,—the element of Secondness in it" (7.659). Furthermore, "even after the percept is formed" Peirce notes that "there is an operation which seems to me to be quite uncontrollable. It is that of judging what it is that the person perceives" (5.115). We must be careful not to draw the wrong conclusion from this and similar claims. One of Peirce's most brilliant insights is a careful distinction between compulsion and authority. A failure to make this distinction leads to the paradoxes of intuitionism where the insistency of a percept or perceptual judgment is mistakenly taken as evidence of the validity or authority of the percept or perceptual judgment. A consequence of this mismating of concepts is that there are basic, infallible, self-authenticating epistemological episodes. This is the error that Peirce claims lies at the core of modern intuitionism, whether it is of the rationalist or empiricist variety.[7] Peirce warns us, "We all know only too well, how terribly insistent perception may be; and yet, for all that, in its most insistent degrees, it may be utterly false,—that is, may not fit into the general mass of experience" (7.647).

Although there are operations of the mind that are uncontrollable, and indeed uncontrollable operations "logically exactly analogous to inferences," inference itself "is essentially deliberate, and self-controlled. . . . Reasoning as deliberate is essentially critical, and it is idle to criticize as good or bad that which cannot be controlled" (5.108). "To criticize as logically sound or unsound an operation of thought that cannot be controlled is not less ridiculous than it would be to pronounce the growth of your hair to be morally good or bad. The ridiculousness in both cases consists in the fact that such a critical judgment may be *pretended* but cannot really be performed in clear thought, for on analysis it will be found absurd" (5.109). But what is it that is controlled in reasoning? It is our habits or conduct. Reasoning involves the use of logic, and "whenever a man reasons, he thinks that he is drawing a conclusion such as would be justified in every analogous case" (5.108). More specifically, all reasoning involves the use of

7. See my article, "Peirce's Theory of Perception," pp. 174 ff.

Action, Conduct, and Self-Control

what Peirce calls "leading" or "guiding" principles. "That which determines us, from given premises, to draw one inference rather than another, is some habit of mind. . . . The particular habit of mind which governs this or that inference may be formulated in a proposition whose truth depends on the validity of the inferences which the habit determines; and such a formula is called a *guiding principle* of inference" (5.367). These guiding principles can be classified into those which are absolutely essential for any reasoning and those material leading principles that are based on experience. Moreover, these guiding principles are involved in warranting the transition from premises to conclusions regardless of whether the type of reasoning is deductive, inductive, or "abductive," the term Peirce uses to name that form of reasoning that leads to new ideas and scientific discovery.

With this conception of rationality as self-control, where our habits and conduct are deliberately controlled, we approach the culmination of Peirce's philosophy. "A rational person . . . not merely has habits, but also can exert a measure of self-control over his future actions" (5.418). He exerts this control by shaping and modifying his conduct which on appropriate occasions issues in specific actions. Self-control is not a matter of "all-or-nothing"; there are degrees of self-control.

> There are inhibitions and coördinations that entirely escape consciousness. There are, in the next place, modes of self-control which seem quite instinctive. Next, there is a kind of self-control which results from training. Next, a man can be his own training-master and thus control his self-control. When this point is reached much or all the training may be conducted in imagination. When a man trains himself, thus controlling control, he must have some moral rule in view, however special and irrational it may be. But next he may undertake to improve this rule; that is, to exercise a control over his control of control. To do this he must have in view something higher than an irrational rule. He must have some sort of moral principle. This, in turn, may be controlled by reference to an esthetic ideal of what is fine. There

are certainly more grades than I have enumerated. Perhaps their number is indefinite. The brutes are certainly capable of more than one grade of control; but it seems to me that our superiority to them is more due to our greater number of grades of self-control than it is to our versatility (5.533).

This rich passage not only enumerates the grades of self-control, it also provides a clue for understanding one of Peirce's most tantalizing suggestions, viz., that there is a hierarchy of the normative sciences such that logic is dependent on ethics and ethics is dependent on esthetics. But before turning to a consideration of the hierarchy of normative sciences, there are further questions to be answered concerning the type of self-control characteristic of rationality.

IV   How are we to analyze self-control? What are its distinguishing features? Self-control "consists (to mention only the leading constituents) first, in comparing one's past deeds with standards, second, in rational deliberation concerning how one will act in the future, in itself a highly complicated operation, third, in the formation of a resolve, fourth, in the creation, on the basis of the resolve, of a strong determination, or modification of habit" (8.320). "Reasoning is essentially a voluntary act, over which we exercise control" (2.144). Self-control demands constant self-criticism. Constant self-criticism is "the very life of reasoning" (2.123). But self-criticism does not take place in a vacuum; self-criticism requires an active community of inquirers, a community that is not completely identified with any existing community, but a community "without definite limits, and capable of a definite increase of knowledge" (5.311). The community of inquirers, which is ultimately the basis for distinguishing the real from the unreal, and the true from the false, functions as a regulative ideal in Peirce's philosophic scheme. (See 5.311.)

Peirce always emphasized the social character of the individual; the very nature of the individual is determined by his forms of participation in community life. "A person is not absolutely an individual. His thoughts are what he is 'saying to himself', that is, is saying to that other self that is just coming into life in the flow of time. When one reasons, it is that critical self that one is trying to persuade; and all thought whatsoever is a sign, and is mostly of the nature of language" (5.421).

The claim that thought is a form of internal dialogue, and that dialogue presupposes a community in which there are effective standards and norms for discourse, is one of Peirce's most fundamental tenets. Peirce also indicated that a "man's circle of society (however widely or narrowly this phrase may be understood), is a sort of loosely compacted person" (5.421). This emphasis on the social or communal nature of man which reflects Peirce's strong anti-subjectivistic and anti-individualistic bias recalls the Platonic and Aristotelian concept of man, and at the same time anticipates the social "forms of life" that play such a prominent role in the later work of Wittgenstein and his followers. It was Plato who first declared that thought is an internal dialogue and Aristotle who stated that man is by nature a social or political animal. And just as Peirce rebelled against the intuitionist and subjectivist tendencies in so much of modern philosophy, so did Wittgenstein. In a variety of ingenious ways, Wittgenstein *shows* what Peirce had *said,* viz., that our language and consequently our thought is embedded in a highly complex context of habits, conventions, and conduct which are social in character (although they may be internalized).

V   Throughout this discussion of conduct, control, criticism, and community, one issue stands out as prominent, the status of norms. There can be no self-control or self-criticism unless there are norms by which we can distinguish the true from the false, the right from the wrong, the correct from the incorrect. All reasoning exists in a logical space of norms. Peirce came to see this point more and more clearly in his mature philosophic outlook. He sought, as we have already suggested, to delineate the essential characteristics of the normative sciences.

A normative science is theoretical and "studies what ought to be" (1.281). Peirce thought that the normative sciences could be exhaustively classified into logic, ethics, and esthetics. The thesis that logic is dependent on ethics may strike us as odd; this thesis seems a complete reversal of the order that we might normally attribute to these disciplines. And the further claim that ethics is dependent on esthetics may strike us as downright absurd. Yet I want to suggest that Peirce's hierarchy of normative disciplines not only embodies a profound insight, but that understanding what he means by this ordering is the key for grasping the import of rationality as self-control. Finally, we will be able to answer the question, What, according to Peirce, is the end or goal of life?

Reasoning, we have seen, is a deliberate form of voluntary conduct that involves the use of logic. Although logic can be divided into different branches, logic is the critique of arguments and especially leading principles. Logic "not only lays down rules which ought to be, but need not be followed; but it is the analysis of the conditions of attainment of something of which purpose is an essential ingredient" (1.575). This latter specification is extremely important because if logic is to lay down rules that ought to be followed in reasoning, then there must be an appeal to an end or purpose by which we can justify the rules that ought to be followed. "Logic is a study of the means of attaining the end of thought" and "it is Ethics which defines that end" (2.198). The dependence of logic on ethics is expressed in other ways. "Thinking is a kind of action, and reasoning is a kind of deliberate action; and to call an argument illogical, or a proposition false, is a special kind of moral judgment" (8.191). "The whole operation of logical self-control takes precisely the same quite complicated course which everybody ought to acknowledge is that of effective ethical self-control" (5.533).

But what is the significance of this thesis that logic is dependent on ethics? Or, making use of the terms "theoretical" and "practical" in the classical sense of these terms, where the "practical" designates the arts of doing and making and the "theoretical" designates the discipline of knowing, we can put the issue in a more general form: What is the point of Peirce's claim that the theoretical is based on the practical? To ask this question is already to indicate the revolutionary quality of Peirce's philosophy, for the dominant tendency in Western philosophy has been to suppose that the theoretical has ultimate primacy over the practical. We must keep in mind that Peirce uses the term "logic" in a variety of ways, but in its broadest sense logic encompasses what we might today call logic, methodology, and theory of knowledge, in short, all reasoning. What Peirce saw so clearly is that all reasoning presupposes norms, and that a comprehensive philosophic system must recognize the primacy of a critique of norms, a critique that examines ultimate ends and purposes. Logic then is a normative discipline, and the discipline from which we evaluate the norms of logic is ethics. We must not think that Peirce is advocating that logic ought to become moralistic; this is a tendency he deplored. But he did believe that the fundamental question of ethics is "What am I prepared deliberately to accept as the statement of what I want to do, what am I to aim at, what am I after?" And logic demands answers to these questions; "it is, therefore, impossible to be thoroughly and rationally logical except on an ethical basis" (2.198). Peirce's insight that all reasoning presupposes norms, that an adequate account of reasoning demands reference to and a critique of norms, has been supported and vindicated by some of the best work in recent analytic philosophy.[8]

When we grapple with the claim that ethics is ultimately based on esthetics, the issue seems to be more perplexing. Not only does this appear to be a more problematic suggestion, but Peirce himself tells us very little about what he means. The supremacy of esthetics is emphasized only in some of Peirce's late papers. Yet I want to suggest that the line of argument that leads him to this conclusion is incisive, crucial for understanding his entire philosophy, and basically sound. If we think of "esthetics" with its normal connotations, rather than its original meaning, we are sure to be misled. By "esthetics" Peirce does not mean a study that is exclusively concerned with understanding and appreciating the nature of such forms of art as painting, sculpture, music, etc. Esthetics is a science of ends, and the business of the esthetician "is to say what is the state of things which is most admirable in itself regardless of any ulterior reason" (1.611). The problem of

8. Cf. Wilfred Sellars, *Science, Perception and Reality* (London, 1963); Roderick Chisholm, *Perceiving* (Ithaca, 1957).

esthetics is "to determine by analysis what it is that one ought deliberately to admire *per se* in itself regardless of what it may lead to and regardless of its bearing upon human conduct" (5.36). From this initial characterization it should be evident that Peirce's view of the object with which esthetics is concerned is closely related to Plato's conception of Good or Καλός and Kant's Ideas of Pure Reason.

Let us try to bring out the significance of the primacy of esthetics by what might seem to be a devious route. I have suggested that there is a parallel to Peirce's claim that logic is based on ethics in recent investigations of norms and rules. But consider for a moment the state of ethical and legal philosophy among Anglo-Saxon philosophers. I believe that Peirce already saw all too clearly what many of these linguistic analysts have failed to see. After the demise of orthodox positivism, and under the inspiration of the later Wittgenstein, we detect a new approach to the problems of ethics and law. Whereas orthodox positivism condemns "ethical judgments" as nonsense, or at best the expression or evincing of noncognitive emotions and attitudes, the newer approach that has replaced positivism has exposed its hidden and unjustified presupposition, viz., that science, or rather what the positivists mistakenly thought of as science, is the measure of all legitimate meaning. Once we saw that the emperor had no clothes, that positivists were telling us what nobody ever doubted—that ethical discourse is different from scientific discourse—a new temper emerged. It was now claimed that ethical discourse is autonomous and that the philosopher's task is to describe the logic of our actual moral discourse with all its intrinsic subtlety and complexity. The new motto became, Moral discourse is rule-regulated discourse! A tremendous amount of intellectual energy has gone into exploring the so-called logic of moral discourse, the ways in which we do argue about moral issues, and the criteria used for distinguishing good and bad reasons in moral arguments. But one of the nagging and persistent questions has been, How are we to provide an ultimate justification for the rules, principles, and norms that we actually do employ? There are some who have suggested that to ask this question is to exceed the bounds of linguistic propriety.

Action, Conduct, and Self-Control

Others recognize this as a legitimate issue, but claim that the philosopher's task is done when he has described moral discourse. Still others, who reveal a hidden affinity with the existentialists, have suggested that, in the end, Decision is king. Even here there has been disagreement about whether such a decision is completely arbitrary (because there are no further standards by which we can evaluate the decisions) or whether such an ultimate decision is the most "rational" decision that a man can make. I think that the entire discussion has floundered because there has been a failure to acknowledge what Peirce saw so well. We cannot be content with a description of our actual moral discourse. No matter how we may attempt to avoid the issue, the question of ultimate justification is crucial. To answer this question we must investigate our ultimate goals and purposes; we must find out what it is that we *ought* ultimately to admire and seek. It is in this sense that ethics is ultimately dependent on esthetics, or to put the issue more neutrally, the criteria of right and wrong in logic as well as in ethics ultimately depend on discovering and acknowledging the end of all human activity. "An ultimate end of action *deliberately* adopted— that is to say, *reasonably* adopted—must be a state of things that *reasonably recommends itself in itself* aside from any ulterior consideration. It must be an *admirable ideal,* having the only kind of goodness that such an ideal *can* have; namely, esthetic goodness. From this point of view the morally good apears as a particular species of the esthetically good" (5.130).

VI   What then is this ultimate ideal? What is the *summum bonum?* What is admirable in itself and has this intrinsic esthetic quality? If action is not the end or goal of human life, what is the end? Peirce answers:

> So, then, the essence of Reason is such that its being never can have been completely perfected. It always must be in a state of incipiency, of growth. It is like the character of a man which consists in the ideas that he will conceive and in the efforts that he will make, and which only develops as the occasions actually arise. . . . The development of Reason requires

Richard J. Bernstein

as a part of it the occurrence of more individual events than ever can occur. It requires, too, all the coloring of all qualities of feeling, including pleasure in its proper place among the rest. The development of Reason consists, you will observe, in embodiment, that is, in manifestation. The creation of the universe, which did not take place during a certain busy week, in the year 4004 B.C., but is going on today and never will be done, is the very development of Reason. *I do not see how one can have a more satisfying ideal of the admirable than the development of Reason so understood. The one thing whose admirableness is not due to an ulterior reason is Reason itself comprehended in all its fullness, so far as we can comprehend it. Under this conception, the ideal of conduct will be to execute our little function in the operation of the creation by giving a hand toward rendering the world more reasonable whenever, as the slang is, it is "up to us" to do so* (my italics; 1.615).

Peirce is not only giving expression to his cosmic vision of the growth of "concrete reasonableness" as *the* ultimate ideal of human life, but also revealing his own deepest personal convictions. This is the ideal by which Peirce himself lived and which enabled him to suffer the pain, misery, and isolation that marred his life. This passage written in 1903 is a conscious formulation of an ideal that Peirce praised much earlier in 1871 when, in speaking of the spirit of Duns Scotus and the scholastics, he said:

Nothing is more striking in either of the great intellectual products of that age, than the complete absence of self-conceit on the part of the artist or philosopher. . . . His work is not designed to embody *his* ideas, but the universal truth. . . . The individual feels his own worthlessness in comparison with his task, and does not dare to introduce his vanity into the doing of it . . . . Finally, there is nothing in which the scholastic philosophy and the Gothic architecture resemble one another more than in the gradually increasing sense of immensity which impresses the mind of the student as he learns to appreciate the real dimensions and cost of each (8.11).

Action, Conduct, and Self-Control

We have come to the very coping stone of Peirce's thought—the ultimate ideal of self-control—the complete commitment to the growth of concrete reasonableness as the *summum bonum*. We have tried to show one path that weaves through an apparent disarray of ideas and themes to this culmination. What initially appears to be confused, chaotic, and even inconsistent, turns out upon analysis systematic, coherent, and powerful. It has always seemed to me that one of the most exciting features of Peirce's work is that the more we try to think out the problems with which he was concerned—problems central to all philosophy—the more we can detect his systematic power. In delineating the connections between the concepts of action, conduct, habit, criticism, community, and control, we have come to the central theme of rationality as self-control, a self-control manifested in a hierarchy of normative sciences where our ultimate ideal, our final end, the *summum bonum,* is the continued growth of concrete reasonableness. The subtlety of Peirce's discussions is evidenced at every turn in this thorny path. And yet, if the systematic network of interlacing concepts that we have sketched is correct, difficulties that we find here in his concept of self-control will reverberate throughout his entire philosophy.

What Peirce's analysis demands at this point is a coherent theory of the self. After all, what is it that exercises the control and is capable of reasonably adopting an ultimate end? Wherein are we to find the identity, unity, and continuity of individual selves? Peirce does not really answer these questions with the same incisiveness that we find in other regions of his philosophy. Despite many important hints, Peirce has failed to work out an adequate theory of the self. Indeed, I believe that this was not only his failure, but the failure of the entire pragmatic movement. We might try to excuse this by recalling the dialectical context in which pragmatism developed. The movement rebelled against the excesses of subjectivism and "mentalism" characteristic of so much modern epistemology. This is not really an excuse, but a way of calling attention to a pervasive failure of this movement. More specifically, I think that there is a serious incoherence in what Peirce does say about the self. We can put the matter this way.

Richard J. Bernstein

We began our exploration of Peirce's philosophy by noting his protest against Hegel. Hegel had failed to take seriously the irreducibility of all three categories. The point is most poignant in relation to Secondness, the category of radical positive individuality. Throughout his intellectual career, Peirce struggled to give proper due to individuality, yet in the final analysis he does not succeed in doing this. He ends—and this comes out clearly in his discussion of the self—where Hegel ended. And the charges that Peirce made against Hegel might well be made against Peirce. Let us see how this is so.

The nature of human individuality always seemed to be a source of intellectual embarrassment for Peirce. He went so far as to claim that "the individual man, since his separate existence is manifested only by ignorance and error, so far as he is anything apart from his fellows, and from what he and they are to be, is only a negation" (5.317). Or again, disparaging radical individuality, he declares, "now you and I—what are we? Mere cells of the social organism. Our deepest sentiment pronounces the verdict of our own insignificance. Psychological analysis shows that there is nothing which distinguishes my personal identity except my faults and my limitations—or if you please, my blind will, which it is my highest endeavor to annihilate" (1.673). There are traces of American transcendentalism and Hegelianism that show up in these passages. But Peirce is betraying his own insight that there is a dimension of radical individuality or positive Secondness that characterizes the individual self. More important, such a conception of the self makes a mockery of the ideal of *individual* self-control or the adoption of the ultimate ideal of concrete reasonableness by an *individual*. If my separate existence is manifested *only* by ignorance and error, if I differ from my fellow man *only* by being a negation, then where is the "I" that controls and adopts ultimate ideals?

VII   It is always a risky matter to relate a man's philosophy to his personal life, and yet there does seem to be an intimate connection between Peirce's failure to develop a positive theory of the self and his personal difficulties. Peirce's first wife remarked,

90

Action, Conduct, and Self-Control

"All his life from boyhood it seems as though everything had conspired to spoil him with indulgence,"[9] and Peirce himself said near the end of his life, "I was brought up with far too loose a rein, except that I was forced to think hard & continuously."[10] He deeply regretted that his father, who brought up Peirce as a prodigy, had "neglected to teach him moral self-control," from which he "suffered unspeakably" throughout his life.[11] Ironically, then, Peirce thought of himself as lacking in the very characteristic that became the coping stone of his philosophy. This might have been a historical curiosity if it were not for the fact that throughout his work there is evidence of a lack of self-control. Despite his brilliance, erudition, subtlety, imagination, and persistence, too often Peirce makes claims that he doesn't justify, or relentlessly pursues some tangential thought, losing sight of his primary concern. This lack of self-control does mar his work, and this deficiency shows up blatantly in his failure to answer those questions concerning the self that his own philosophy requires.

But, as we have already noted, self-control and self-criticism are intimately bound up with the existence of an active community of inquirers that carries on persistent and thorough dialogue. Peirce, whose work is far in advance of his time, and whose personal idiosyncrasies offended many of his contemporaries, was virtually ostracized from the "intellectual" community. He suffered what is perhaps the worst form of punishment for a philosopher, especially one who made the "community of inquirers" a cardinal principle of his philosophy, condemnation by silence. The forces of mediocrity, conservatism, and stupidity ignored and nearly crushed the spirit of America's foremost philosopher. The most fitting tribute that we can pay to Peirce is for each of us to help make the community of inquirers a living presence and to engrave on our souls his plea never to block the road of inquiry.

9. Quoted in Murray G. Murphey, *The Development of Peirce's Philosophy* (Cambridge, Mass., 1961), p. 17.
10. *Letters to Lady Welby,* ed. Irwin C. Lieb (New Haven, 1953), p. 37.
11. See Introduction, p. 9.

Chapter 4   Community and Reality

John E. Smith

Charles Sanders Peirce was at once a genuine and a disturbing philosopher. He was genuine because he dealt directly with the difficult problems of philosophy: the nature of truth, the theory of reality, the problems of mind and of God. In his approach there was none of the modern or advanced tendency in thought that anticipates speculative problems merely in order to avoid them or to dissolve them into the misadventures of human speech. Peirce is disturbing because he forces us to confront experience afresh, and if need be to revise our categories so that they will accord with the real world. If you study Peirce you have to be prepared for surprises; you have to be tough-minded enough to consider the possibility that things may in fact prove to be very different from the way you have long since decided that they *must* be.

The secret of Peirce's greatness as a philosopher—a greatness we are only now beginning to appreciate—lies in the skill with which he combined openness to experience with logical acumen and the ability to develop a comprehensive and coherent system. His empiricism has long been understood; his ability and his success as a systematic, speculative philosopher have been underestimated. In an earlier paper on Peirce[1] I quite mistakenly described him as *not* being a systematic philosopher after the fashion of Hegel. In this I was deceived. While I never underestimated

---

1. "Religion and Theology in Peirce," *Studies in the Philosophy of Charles Sanders Peirce*, ed. P. P. Wiener and F. H. Young (Cambridge, Mass., 1952), pp. 251–67.

the metaphysical and even theological bent of his thought, I did confound the form in which his writings have come to us with the logical structure of his thought. I took the fact that in order to discover Peirce's theory on a given topic one has to plow through volumes of papers, drafts and revisions of drafts, reviews, and partially completed manuscripts, to mean a lack of system. It is now clear to me that this was an error. Peirce has a metaphysical system of remarkable scope, and on any given topic there is a clear drift to his thought even if he did not make it easy for us to find it out. In view of this fact, I want to treat his view of reality in systematic fashion and as a matter of principle. I shall not undertake to trace his intellectual odyssey through the customary early, middle, and late writings. This task may be left to intellectual historians and to the guardians of Peirce's papers. Instead I shall treat Peirce's theory of reality as an integral position sufficiently clear and unified to form a distinctive alternative to other philosophical outlooks.[2]

My chief aim is twofold: first, to present Peirce's theory of reality, involving as it does the idea of a community of inquirers or knowers, and second, to offer some critical appraisal of its consistency and adequacy. In seeking to achieve the first aim it will be necessary to mark out the distinctively realistic, idealistic, and pragmatic strains in the theory and then to show how he synthesized these strains in an original way. In seeking to achieve the second aim, I shall adapt a device used by Peirce himself. Just after the turn of the century, Peirce wrote several reviews of Josiah Royce's Gifford Lectures, *The World and the Individual,* and it is evident that he regarded Royce's view as the most serious rival of his own. Without becoming too deeply involved in academic discussion, I shall seek to evolve a final appraisal of Peirce's view from a crucial comparison with that of Royce.

---

2. Peirce was a meticulous thinker and never one to omit detail. This means that there are subtleties and qualifications in his view on every topic; they make it especially difficult to consider any of his ideas in brief compass. Tributes to Peirce, however, must be limited even if Peirce's attention to detail and the number of his papers were not.

THE GENERAL THEORY OF REALITY

In Peirce's manuscripts and notes for his projected work on logic of 1873, we find a discussion of the concept of reality that will serve as a start. This discussion nicely brings out the several strands in the theory and it is largely in agreement with the many other characterizations he offered of the meaning of reality. He starts by asking how a variety of observations and processes of thought can lead ultimately to a settled conclusion that is accepted by all who understand what is meant. The fact that diverse thinkers agree in a common result is not to be taken simply as a brute fact; on the contrary, the convergence of many observations, ideas, views in a common object stands in need of explanation. At the outset Peirce freely admits that the theory according to which external realities *cause* the common result and belief in one identical object can serve as an explanation. The causal theory, he says, is "convenient for certain purposes" (7.335) and is without internal logical flaw. But he has a philosophical objection to that theory; what needs to be explained, he says, is not an ordinary event among others in the world, and it cannot be put in the same class with such events. The fact that investigation leads to a fixed result concerns the theory of truth; the logic of investigation and its outcome, though related to fact, is itself a matter of principle not to be treated after the fashion of singular occurrences in the course of nature. The point is an important one, for while Peirce was vigorous in his insistence that reality has force, power, resistance (what he called Secondness) over against ideas and representations, he still refused to accept a simple, causal theory of knowledge and truth.

If a causal theory will not suffice, some further explanation is required. This is furnished by Peirce's theory of reality as the ultimate result of inquiry. It is best to begin with a summary statement of Peirce's view and then seek to unfold its meaning in more detail by elucidating its constituent aspects. Since Peirce gave expression to his theory in so many places it will be necessary to select several quotations as standard. I believe that Peirce was not entirely consistent in the statement of the theory, but we must be careful not to take a difference in accent for a difference in viewpoint. "The real is that which is not whatever we happen to think it, but is unaffected by what we may think of it" (8.12). Or again, the real is "that whose characters are independent of what anybody may think them to be" (5.405). Still further, Peirce speaks of reality as what a community of investigators is destined to discover if they have the proper method of inquiry and persist far enough in its application: "the opinion which is fated to be ultimately agreed to by all who investigate, is what we mean by the truth, and the object represented in this opinion is the real" (5.407). Finally, "reality is independent, not necessarily of thought in general, but only of what you or I or any finite number of men may think about it . . . though the object of the final opinion depends on what that opinion is, yet what that opinion is does not depend on what you or I or any man thinks" (5.408).

These passages give expression to the essentials of Peirce's theory, although, as we shall see, they must be supplemented by others. Three ideas are dominant in the passages we have cited: first, the idea that reality has some sort of *independence* of being thought or represented; second, the idea that reality is related to thought and ideas in some essential way; and third, the idea that reality is the ultimate result of a process of inquiry and is in some sense to be identified with the fact that those who conduct the inquiry come to believe or accept this result. Those acquainted with the development of modern philosophy will see at once that Peirce was deliberately trying to combine elements and characteristics that have generally been regarded as mutually exclusive. Using the labels of philosophical schools, it seems that Peirce wanted to be at once a realist, an idealist, and a pragmatist. And indeed this is the case. The problem is to see whether Peirce was able to construct a coherent theory from such normally divergent tendencies. We must consider in more detail each of the three ideas in question, and then we shall be in a position to grasp the full scope of Peirce's view.

(1) Reality and Independence

In many passages Peirce claims that being real means that a thing retains its characters regardless of what particular men may think (1.578; 3.161; 5.405, 5.408, 5.503; 6.495; 7.339; 8.12). That this independence of thought does not mean independence of thought in general, but only of particular thoughts, is a point to which we shall return. For the present we may concentrate on independence because that aspect marks the realistic strain in Peirce's thought. Unlike Hegel, who emphasized the utter transparence of all reality to reason, Peirce was insistent on the *forcefulness* or otherness of things as a mark of reality. In Peirce's terminology, reality belongs with Secondness, or the domain of fact. "The reality of things consists in their persistent forcing themselves upon our recognition" (1.175); or again, "In the idea of reality, Secondness is predominant; for the real is that which insists upon forcing its way to recognition as something *other* than the mind's creation" (1.325). The real is what demands our attention, and on more than one occasion Peirce interpreted the human phenomenon of *willing* as our response to the insistence of what stands over against us (1.381; cf. 1.358, 1.325; 3.337, 3.613).

In order to avoid confusion it is essential to notice the difference between reality and the real. This is not a pedantic distinction, but rather a mark of Peirce's subtlety. The real in the sense of the thing, the idea, the feeling, has the status of fact; it is what reveals itself in action and reaction with other things. Sometimes Peirce says that the real thing is what exists, but we must be careful in using this formulation because Peirce generally refused to identify reality with what is existent or actual. The important point is that *what* is real is itself a something or other that has forcefulness and insistence. On the other hand, we do not entirely answer the question of what it means to be real merely by pointing to real things. Reality is the status enjoyed by real things, and, as such, its meaning cannot be grasped apart from a theory. We may summarize by saying that the real thing is marked by Secondness or forcefulness and power, whereas the theory of reality is a matter of Thirdness or of thought, and this involves something more than the ability to react with other things.

There are at least two other ways in which Peirce expresses what we have called the realistic pole or the independence of the real thing over against thought. One is his concept of the index or indexical sign, and the other is the doctrine of the dynamical object. Time and again Peirce argued that it is impossible to distinguish between the real world and a fictitious or imaginary one by means of a general description (2.337; 3.363; 8.39 ff.). Expressed in terms of the theory of signs, this means that every assertion must contain at least one index designating the real subject matter about which assertions are made. Armed with predicates alone, or universals, we are unable to reach the real world; unless we begin with a designated real subject no dialectic of inquiry will produce such a subject. As Peirce says, no language contains a general indicator telling us that we are now talking about the real world; we either know already that our discussion is about such a world or we must be content to talk about fictions or merely to play games with words. In our conversations we may succeed in commanding attention to realities by our tone of voice or the seriousness of our demeanor, but unless it is thus understood at the outset that we mean to refer to a real subject matter there is no purely logical movement within the sphere of thought that will suffice to distinguish talk about an imaginary world from talk about the only real world there is.

Peirce used this line of argument against Royce in his review of Royce's early book, *The Religious Aspect of Philosophy*. There Royce had claimed that we reach the individual, the real subject, only at the point where full and perfect knowledge—complete determination—has been achieved. For reasons not germane to our purpose, Royce was bound to hold that, as long as we have nothing more than partial knowledge, we are unable to identify the individual or real subject of our assertions. Peirce objected vigorously, claiming that this view entirely ignores the function of the index[3] in providing a real subject at the outset of inquiry, although Peirce

3. See 8.39 ff.; in view of Royce's great debt to Kant, it is ironical that Peirce should accuse him of passing over Kant's view of space and time as forms of

betrays the idealist flavor of his position by taking this index to mean the *will* that forces attention. It may, of course, be objected to Peirce's view in turn that, in continuing to define the real object through the manner in which it is indicated, he fails to sustain a realist position. On the other hand, it is clear that Peirce refuses (at least in this argument) to identify the real by means of any description, not even a complete or final one. We have yet to see whether this refusal is consistent with his theory of reality as the ultimate opinion destined to be arrived at by the community of investigators.

One further expression of the realistic pole is found in the concept of the dynamical object. We normally think of an idea or sign as representing an object to be of a certain character, and we say that when the idea is adequate the object is as the idea determines it to be. Peirce accepts this, but he distinguishes between the object as thought or the *immediate* object and the object that exerts itself in relation to other objects or the *dynamical* object. The immediate object is dependent on the sign, but the dynamical object reverses the relationship, because "[the dynamical object] is the Reality which by some means contrives to determine the Sign to its Representation" (4.536). The dynamical object is thus no mere object of thought, but rather a source of effects; it is a dynamic center which has constraining power over the sign that is to represent it. The stubborn character of the dynamical object is one of the factors that enter into the process of inquiry and help to justify the claim that the process will arrive at a stable result independent of particular thoughts (cf. 5.503).

Thus far nothing has been said about Peirce's famous Scotistic, or scholastic, realism. The reason for the omission may be explained. The philosophical realism, which Peirce frequently attributed to Duns Scotus and sometimes to the scholastic tradition, generally embraces two theses:[4] (1) reality includes what is general,

---

intuition guaranteeing individuality as distinct from categories that function as predicates and are thus insufficient for providing a real subject.

4. See 5.543 for a succinct statement; the Scotistic realism is mentioned in many places where it is invariably contrasted with nominalism.

and (2) reality includes the vague and real possibilities. The former thesis is intended to be a denial of the claim that reality is exhausted by wholly actual individuals entirely contained in a present moment of time, and the latter is intended to be a denial of the view that mere possibility is a blank nothingness. Now while it is certainly true that these realistic theses are relevant to and indeed form part of Peirce's theory of reality, it is not correct to identify what I have been calling the realistic pole in Peirce's theory with the so-called Scotistic realism. For the realistic pole concerns primarily the matter of the independence of the real as over against thought and representation, whereas the Scotistic realism is concerned chiefly with the reality of the general, and the denial of the modern view that reality is made up entirely of sensible particulars. Scotistic realism figures most prominently in Peirce's general theory of reality at the point where it becomes necessary to defend the real possibility that attaches to possible or future experience. As we shall see, the status of the ultimate opinion that "would be" discovered by the community of inquirers upon fulfillment of the relevant conditions depends upon Peirce's doctrine of real possibility, which is the heart of the Scotistic realism.

(2) Reality and Thought in General

That there is a strong idealistic strain in Peirce's philosophy cannot be denied; whether his theory of reality as such is to be described as thoroughly idealistic is a question more difficult to answer. We may postpone this question and concentrate on the idealistic element. Three considerations are essential. The first, and most obvious, is Peirce's own description of his thought as idealistic. Secondly, there is the close connection to be found in every phase of Peirce's thought between signs and representation —in his terminology, Thirdness—and the real object. Finally, there is the definition of reality in terms of opinion and belief, together with the claim that the real is not external to or independent of thought in general.

As regards the first point, Peirce associated his view with a form

99

of Hegelianism (1.42), and described objective idealism as "the one intelligible theory of the universe" (6.25, cf. 6.102). In several places (e.g. 5.358 n.) Peirce referred to Royce's *World and the Individual* as generally correct, and in a letter to William James (8.284) he called his own pragmaticism the "true idealism." Although we must not depend too heavily on self-conscious interpretation of this sort, the fact remains that Peirce was extraordinarily circumspect in the expression of his views, and, as should now be clear, he was at least as reliable a commentator on Peirce as any member of the Charles Peirce Society!

With regard to the status of signs, thought, and representation, it is clear that Peirce viewed them as belonging to the nature of the real.[5] Thirdness in the sense of law and meaning (including both the *meaning* of terms and *meaning* to do some act or other) has its own reality and cannot be reduced to Firstness and Secondness. Thirdness, moreover, cannot be derived from the relation between Firstness (quality) and Secondness (fact), or indeed from any dyadic relation. The relation, however, between Thirdness and the real object is not so clear, and Peirce has made statements about that relationship that are certainly paradoxical, and in the end inconsistent with each other. The idealistic element predominates on most occasions.

5. Peirce upheld an essentially idealistic interpretation of signs and the function of representation. While it is not true that all instances of Thirdness require the notion of mind (see, for example, 1.366), Peirce almost invariably mentioned intention and the ability to represent as a mental activity in his discussions of signs and triadic relations (1.420, 1.475; 5.292, 5.287). The various attempts that have been made to reduce Peirce's theory to a form of behaviorism remain unsuccessful because genuine Thirdness and intellectual purport are never identical with actual behavior. Thirdness, in the sense of sign and law connecting phenomena, is indeed related to public fact, overt act, and external events, but there is always generality in Thirdness, and generality—a form of intellectual purport—cannot be exhausted in any fact or finite collection of facts. Moreover, the attempt to equate Thirdness with habit raises the same difficulty. For while Peirce did connect Thirdness intimately with habit, and thus did not confine himself to a narrow, "mentalistic" conception of mind as merely immediate consciousness, habit itself cannot be understood apart from generality or general tendency to continue in a certain pattern. Like intellectual purport, habit is never adequately analyzed into actual behavior.

Community and Reality

There is, Peirce says, nothing that is incognizable in principle. There is no "thing in itself," and while it is not the case that everything is in fact known, everything real is knowable, and there is no transcendence of the object of knowledge. Peirce says (8.13) that the view of reality to which he is sympathetic is one that is "fatal to the idea of . . . a thing existing independent of all relation to the mind's conception of it" (cf. 5.311). Or again, in criticizing Royce, he says, "We do not aim at anything quite beyond experience, but only at the limiting result toward which all experience will approximate" (8.112). Peirce goes on to characterize the view as one that "eliminates any non-notional correlate of knowledge" (8.112). This all sounds like philosophical idealism, a conclusion that is reinforced by Peirce's definition of reality in terms of belief or opinion.

Over against what has just been said, however, stand Peirce's most puzzling attacks upon idealism. It is as if, in the development of his own pragmaticism, Peirce felt free to express the idealism in it without apology, but that in the face of a thoroughgoing idealist like Royce he felt constrained to advance realism as if its truth were a foregone conclusion. One cannot but acknowledge the extreme tension in Peirce's thought at this point. On the one hand, we find him saying that without thought there can be no opinion, and hence no final opinion such as would serve to identify reality. Hence the real cannot be external to mind. On the other hand, we find him attacking Royce in the most vigorous terms for failing to see that *to be* and *to be represented* are not the same. In one place (8.130) we even find Peirce arguing that realism as a philosophical position is a matter of fact, and that it neither can nor need be made a matter of demonstration. "The question of realism," he says, "is a question of hard fact, if ever there was a hard fact," so that the realist escapes the need to establish his position by the sort of dialectic illustrated in Royce's *World and the Individual*. Peirce was no doubt goaded by the polemical intent. Royce had attempted to fasten upon realism the extreme thesis that "to be is to be independent of an idea"—where "independent" is taken as symmetrical—so that if the thing is independent of the idea or representation, the idea or representation is equally in-

101

dependent of the thing. The result is that the idea may vary in any way or to any extent you please without ceasing to be a representation of the intended object. Peirce took this consequence to be absurd. We need not settle the question of the correctness of Royce's interpretation of realism to see that his rejection of it in such extreme form led Peirce to bring out all the realistic elements in his own position. I am inclined to think that Peirce's position was in fact determined to a greater extent by dialectical relation to other views than he was willing to allow (cf. 8.126).

We turn now to the third outcropping of Peirce's idealism as expressed in the fundamental doctrine that reality is to be defined in terms of an opinion or belief. The pragmatistic aspects of this doctrine—the nature of inquiry, the community of investigators, and the probabilistic interpretation of synthetic reasoning—will be considered in the next section. Here emphasis will fall upon the fact that reality is said to coincide with an opinion, a belief, a system of propositions that represent the ultimate outcome of inquiry. Our question here concerns the extent to which the real is dependent upon thought or representation, and whether reality has transcendence over being known. It is well to bear in mind that, while Peirce explicitly denied the identification of being with being represented, the question of the precise relation between the two remains open. The denial of identity all by itself means no more than that the two items in question are "other than" each other in at least one specifiable respect. But while being and being represented may be other and not identical, it may be the case that one is dependent on the other so that the relation is asymmetrical. In short, the denial of identity does not tell us enough, for, as will become apparent, Peirce believed that he could deny the identity of being and being represented without also holding that the real is entirely independent of representation.

Whatever inconsistencies there may be in Peirce's theory, one idea is expressed repeatedly, namely, that reality is independent of what is thought by this, that, or the other individual, and even of any finite collection of individuals, but that it is not independent of thought in general. Peirce's position, that is to say, ulti-

Community and Reality

mately takes shape as an *objective* idealism in which the rational pole is purged of any hint of subjectivism or privacy in belief by the rigorous control of the method of inquiry. I would regard as atypical the well-known statement in Peirce's exposition of the "social theory of logic" in which he refers to the "ideal perfection of knowledge" as that by which "reality is constituted" (5.356). The reason why this assertion cannot be taken at face value is found in the many points at which Peirce himself finds it necessary to distinguish the object represented from the opinion that represents it, and even from the ultimate opinion that can be only in the future (see 8.103 ff.). It is not consistent with all the realistic passages in Peirce's writings to say that for him knowledge *constitutes* reality. The identification is too strong, and would mean that Secondness, in the sense of the dynamic element that is not cognitional, had been eliminated and everything reduced to Thirdness; this is precisely the error with which Peirce charged Hegel. On the other hand, reality is defined through opinion and thought; there is no modifying that fact and no valid way of explaining it away. The fact is, and this is the crux of Peirce's entire philosophy, that he believed it defensible to connect reality essentially with thought as long as the thought in question is of a certain ultimate character that does not depend upon finite thinkers who, taken singly, are fallible and without final authority (see especially 8.14). The thought or opinion that defines reality must therefore belong to a *community* of knowers, and this community must be structured and disciplined in accordance with super-individual principles. Moreover, it is not possible to minimize the idealism implicit in this conclusion by attempting to interpret thought, opinion, belief in a behavioristic way. For an opinion is thought, and thought means Thirdness; Thirdness has its own being and is never identical with any action, any fact or finite collection of facts. The final estimation of Peirce's position must be one that takes his idealism seriously and interprets it as such. Whatever shortcomings there may be in Peirce's theory cannot be overcome by the device of translating thought into something other than itself.

(3) Reality and Community

Here the chief aim is to complete Peirce's theory of reality by developing the pragmatistic elements in it; in so doing we must also indicate how he believed it possible to combine the realistic and idealistic poles in his thought. The real is what is disclosed through the application of empirical method; it is also called the stable belief expressed in that ultimate opinion resulting, in the long run, from the persistent following of the method of science. The doctrine is a complex one and contains several distinct ideas, each of which forms a topic in its own right. We may cite a few typical statements: "When we busy ourselves to find the answer to a question, we are going upon the hope that there is an answer, which can be called *the* answer, that is, the final answer . . . which sufficient inquiry will compel us to accept" (4.61); "the real is the idea in which the community ultimately settles down" (6.610); "The opinion which is fated to be ultimately agreed to by all who investigate, is what we mean by the truth, and the object represented in this opinion is the real" (5.407); "the validity of an inductive argument consists, then, in the fact that it pursues a method which, if duly persisted in, must, in the very nature of things, lead to a result indefinitely approximating to the truth in the long run" (2.781); "the real, then, is that which, sooner or later, information and reasoning would finally result in, and which is therefore independent of the vagaries of me and you . . . the very origin of the conception of reality shows that this conception essentially involves the notion of a COMMUNITY" (5.311); and finally, "in addition to actuality and possibility, a *third* mode of reality must be recognized in that which, as the gipsy fortune-tellers express it, is 'sure to come true', or, as we may say, is *destined*" (4.547); "anything may fairly be said to be *destined* which is sure to come about although there is no necessitating reason for it" (4.547 n. 1).[6]

---

6. I purposely omit from the list of passages cited those (such as 5.351–52) that raise, or seem to raise, the question as to whether there is anything real at all. Peirce's entire philosophy is oriented to the problem of coming to know

Community and Reality

From the above statements of the community theory of reality we must extract, for more detailed scrutiny, the following notions: (1) belief or opinion as a goal of inquiry; (2) serious inquiry governed by the form of synthetic reasoning; (3) the community of inquirers; (4) convergence of belief destined in the long run; and (5) the mode of real possibility, or the "would-be." It is obvious that each of these topics demands extended treatment that is out of the question in the present context, and yet the main subject—Peirce's theory of reality—cannot be understood apart from these topics. Attention, therefore, must be confined to absolute essentials.

(1) *Belief or opinion as the goal of inquiry* For Peirce, the human mind is neither fixed nor static; it is a most complex set of powers and capacities that stand related to a unified person seeking to live a purposeful life in an evolving universe. The mind moves between the poles of doubt and belief. The former is marked by uneasiness, restlessness, and hesitation in overt action; when we are in doubt we are not sure how to move. Belief, on the other hand, means confidence, resolution, and that sort of adjustment or ease in behavior or response that we all recognize in our habitual actions. Between doubt and belief stands inquiry. Doubt is not a resting place; we seek to move away from the uneasiness of doubt to the stability of belief. Inquiry, investigation, testing, experience, experiment are all names for the middle term, the means or bridge over which we are to pass from doubt to belief.

Peirce was well aware that in actual fact men often believe what is not true or warranted and often refuse to believe what is true. He was, moreover, too steeped in his own empiricist cast of mind not to know that men have ways of arriving at and maintaining their beliefs that are not in accord with the way of experience and the scientific temper he recommended. Peirce never maintained that in fact everyone does fix his belief as a result of well-disci-

---

and to justify our knowledge of what there is; he is not primarily concerned with the question: Is there anything to know? That is to say that Peirce does not belong to that school of philosophers who start with language, thoughts, sensory data, and then go on to ask *whether* there is an external world.

plined inquiry based on objective evidence and careful reasoning. But Peirce did believe that, unless a man succeeded in remaining isolated, utterly independent, prejudiced, and confined to his own private opinion, he would in the long run come to believe the warranted results of objective inquiry. Peirce was, in short, a hopeless idealist in this regard; for him the course of the universe guarantees this happy dissemination of the truth.

Peirce, as we have seen, identifies reality by means of a certain type of belief. The real is that which is represented through and meant by a warranted opinion. What is must be represented in an opinion or belief before we can speak about truth. Things might be, to be sure, without ever being said to be true in our human sense, but we could not know this to be the case. Knowledge, in short, introduces belief, ideas, and opinions. The problem, as Peirce saw it, is not to lay hold of what is in the paradoxical sense of what is apart from all relation to belief and opinion, but to lay hold of the real through the only medium of its disclosure to finite human beings, namely, ideas and opinions. But the opinion that defines the real must have an extra-human character about it.

For our purpose it is not necessary to settle the matter of the full meaning Peirce attached to belief, its relation to action, to habit, and to concepts or intellectual purport. Whatever belief may turn out to mean in Peirce's view, it is still essentially connected with reality. That belief is not identical with action or behavior in his view is now generally admitted. Peirce did not dissolve reality into human functionings as pragmatism is generally supposed to have done. But he does hold that reality cannot be utterly independent of the objective conditions according to which warranted opinion comes about. This is his pragmatic idealism.

(2) *Serious inquiry governed by the form of synthetic reasoning* It is obvious that if we are to have a warranted belief going beyond the mere fact that some opinion is believed, there must be a basis for the warrant. This basis is supplied by the *method* of inquiry and the theory of induction or synthetic reasoning, or the process of extending knowledge of real things as "the lock upon the door

of philosophy" (5.348). The problem of understanding science is at one with the problem of finding some law or pattern in the development of new belief from old belief and fresh experience. That form of reasoning is justified that tends on the whole and in the long run to lead to "certain predestinate conclusions which are the same for all men" (3.161). For Peirce, science in the sense of a method for arriving at conclusions rather than in the sense of a systematic form of presenting them is the embodiment of inductive procedure.

It is clear from the many discussions of induction and the nature of science offered by Peirce at every stage of his development that the ground or warrant for a concluding opinion is always the *method* by which it has been reached. Inquiry, that is to say, has a logical structure so that any proposed result of inquiry finds its ultimate justification in its relation to that structure. Serious inquiry aimed at acquiring knowledge of the real world as distinct from fictitious or imaginary universes starts with the assumption that there is an answer, *the* answer to the question that directs the process. Moreover, there is the further assumption that this answer would be found if the inquiry persisted. Empirical inquiry means the application of synthetic reasoning or induction. Without becoming deeply involved in Peirce's account of probability, we may say that such justification as induction receives at his hands takes the form of a large circle of explanation. On the one hand, he holds that the principle of induction[7] cannot be given a deductive foundation (2.693) and cannot be based on the celebrated "uniformity of nature." This view is in accord with his claim (5.341 ff.) that we need no logical ground for logicality itself beyond a large proportion of successes in actual inquiry. On the other hand, he says:

> that the rule of induction will hold good in the long run may
> be deduced from the principle that reality is only the object

7. In most cases Peirce takes this principle to be the inference from a known part or sample of a class to all other members not yet experienced. In 5.341 an alternative formulation of the principle of induction is: How is it that when some facts are true, other facts standing in a special relation to them are also true?

of the final opinion to which sufficient investigation would lead. That belief gradually tends to fix itself under the influence of inquiry is, indeed, one of the facts with which logic sets out (2.693).

Whether Peirce's solution of the problem of induction is successful or not is a matter of lesser importance for our purpose than the fact that in his view the warrant for belief resides in the *form* of inquiry and not in the predilections, interests, or other beliefs that can be ascribed to those who accept the results of inquiry. It would therefore be more in accord with Peirce's intention to say that reality, insofar as it is identified through the ultimate belief resulting from inquiry, is defined by a *form* of rationality rather than by the fact of a belief's being held. And even if Peirce did on occasion regard the fact that the result of inquiry compels belief as the pragmatic way of understanding reality, it still remains true that it is the *logical warrant* for the belief, and not the fact of believing, that is the important factor. In short, his pragmaticism, despite the emphasis on practice, is quite rationalistic.

(3) *The community of inquirers*   Enough has already been said to make it clear that—for Peirce—the process of knowledge is no merely individual affair. The idea that scientific inquiry requires many individuals and is a cooperative undertaking stems from two sources. One is to be found in Peirce's rejection of absolutely immediate cognition or intuition, and the other is in his extensive knowledge of natural science.

From a logical point of view, the claim that every cognition is fallible means that every cognition is subject to review, confirmation, correction, or rejection by some subsequent cognition. The heart of the experimental approach is found in critical testing of hypotheses so that no idea or opinion taken in isolation and apart from an experimental process can be accepted as expressing the truth. In order to criticize a given perception or theory, we must appeal to another. In rejecting the tradition of intuitive rationalism initiated in modern philosophy by Descartes, Peirce allied himself with the Hegelian approach, according to which truth can be attained only through an organic process that is dialectical in the sense that it involves a gradual criticism of what is merely private or subjective, and the preservation of the objective and universal. The process is too vast to be confined to the experience and thought of any single individual, and in any case each individual must be subject to a standard transcending his own ideas. Moreover, the individual himself is a microcosm of the community since his own personal experience and thought involve him in a continual dialogue and dialectic of ideas. To obtain a critical result it is necessary to compare, contrast, and correct our ideas, and especially to test them in the stream of experience. No one of these operations of thought is immediate or intuitive, but each requires a *series* of ideas and logical operations that takes us continually beyond the boundary of any single or isolated idea. It is important to notice that the community principle means both a community of inquirers or knowers and a community or system of ideas.

Peirce regarded the idea of the community as essential for the understanding of science. This fact throws further light on the theory of reality, because that theory may be interpreted as an extension and analogy of the convergence of opinion that Peirce found to be characteristic of scientific inquiry. The use of natural science as a model is readily understood as soon as we recall that Peirce had an extensive knowledge of actual scientific procedure and was engaged throughout his life in scientific work of his own. Peirce was in touch with science in the making, and that is precisely the feature he continually emphasized in his many writings on science and scientific method. For Peirce, science is primarily an activity or actual process of inquiry; it is only secondarily a systematic body of results. Although Peirce was second to none in the ability to analyze what is sometimes called the logical structure of science, he would not agree that science can be understood apart from the actual process of inquiry. Science, as he saw it, means an actual attack by a community of actual investigators on an actual problem posed by some actual subject matter. Progress depends on communication, comparison, and criticism of results. The work of science is not achieved by any individual or group alone, but only by the cooperation of many individuals and groups.

The emphasis on cooperative endeavor naturally raises the question of the nature of the community. For Peirce, the attainment of critical conclusions requires that each individual investigator be capable of transcending his private interests and opinions. The community of investigators purporting to be scientific is defined by the willingness of each individual member to sacrifice what is personal and private to him alone in order to follow the dictates of an interpersonal method that involves free exchange of views and results. "In storming the stronghold of truth, one mounts upon the shoulders of another who has to ordinary apprehension failed, but has in truth succeeded by virtue of the lessons of his failure" (7.51). The cumulative results of investigation are preserved by the community. The community idea is not a mere metaphor, nor does it stand as but a piece of rhetoric in praise of science; the idea belongs to the logical structure of scientific activity. Not everyone who investigates is a scientific inquirer, but only those who are cognizant of and willing to bind themselves to empirical method. In this way alone can there come into being knowledge of a real world that is "independent of the vagaries of me and you" (5.311).

The idea of science as an activity engaged in by a community of inquirers, and the conception of reality as an ultimate opinion reached by this process of inquiry, are reciprocal notions. On one side we have the idea of the real as an ultimate opinion which is, though not external to thought in general, still independent of what this, that, or the other individual thinker may happen to think. On the other side we have the idea of the method for reaching such an opinion that requires individual inquirers to constitute themselves as members of the community of science through their willingness to sacrifice their privacy and bind themselves by the rules of an interpersonal method.

(4) *Convergence of belief destined in the long run*   In the foregoing account of science and empirical method two features have been omitted; each is vital and in some ways both are more important than all the rest. One is the idea that processes of inquiry tend to converge to a limit or stable and ultimate belief; the other con-

cerns the mode of real possibility through which Peirce interprets what "would be" the result of a process extended in the "long run."

Peirce believed that every controlled process of inquiry if persisted in tends to issue in a stable result that establishes itself as *the* answer to the question of the inquiry. This stable result means at the same time the exclusion of all other views on the matter. Peirce offers two reasons for this conclusion. On the empirical side he cites the evidence of the history of science: persistent inquiry actually produces a limiting opinion or narrowing interval within which belief never ceases to oscillate. On the logical side there is the theory of probability and Peirce's evolutionary metaphysics according to which the entire universe exhibits a drift toward rationality or order in habits.[8] The history of science shows that questions actually do get answered, and the logic of inquiry shows that in the long run all questions would be answered.

What are we to understand by Peirce's repeated claim that the ultimate stable belief defining the reality of this or that is *destined* to come about, and what empirical meaning are we to attach to the concept of the long run? The community of inquirers is said to be constrained in some way to reach a final belief that is destined, but this is to happen only if favorable conditions continue to prevail and the inquiry persists in the "long run." To say that a belief is destined to result is to say that a certain opinion *would be* arrived at in the long run. The claim assumes that the method of inductive inquiry is reliable, that it is "a method which, if duly persisted in, must, in the very nature of things, lead to a result indefinitely approximating to the truth in the long run" (2.781). The constraining element implied in the term "destiny" Peirce elucidates through the example of throwing a pair of dice. If we throw the dice often enough sixes will be sure to turn up, although

8. One of the liabilities of treating a comprehensive topic in a brief paper is found in the need to omit what should not be left out of account. Peirce's evolutionary cosmology as expressed in the doctrines of Tychism (Chance), Synechism (Continuity) and Agapism (Evolutionary Love) should be brought in as part of his general theory of reality. Moreover, a thorough consideration of his theory of habit is also needed for the proper understanding of the "would-be," or mode of reality that stands between actual fact and logical possibility.

there is no necessitating reason that they should. By analogy this means that the real universe in which inquiry takes place is such that the ultimate opinion is sure to come about at some time, although there is no necessitating reason for this and there is no certainty that in fact the opinion has been reached at this or that particular time (see especially 4.547 n.).

Peirce is pointing to a state of affairs that falls somewhere between the extremes of accident and mechanical necessity. What is destined to come has *some* constraining or rational form in it so that it is neither haphazard nor wholly fortuitous, and yet on the other hand what is destined does not come about with the brute necessity of a self-repeating system. The element of rationality behind the destiny resides in the *method* that determines the activity of the community of investigators. In speaking of the active work of scientists, Peirce says:

> the progress of investigation carries them by a force outside themselves to one and the same conclusion . . . This activity of thought by which we are carried, not where we wish, but to a fore-ordained goal, is like the operation of destiny. No modification of the point of view taken, no selection of other facts for study, no natural bent of mind even, can enable a man to escape the predestinate opinion (5.407).

This Calvinistic logic means apparently that the outcome is inevitable but not necessary! Peirce was, of course, aware of the need to suppose the continuation of favorable conditions. The reaching of the predestinate opinion is favored both by the nature of the universe and the form of inquiry, but neither would suffice unless there were also a dedicated community of inquirers loyal to the spirit of science. If the race were to be extinguished or if interest in inquiry no longer existed or if empirical method were abandoned, the predestinate opinion would remain undiscovered.

In addition to what has already been said about the goal of inquiry, there is the fact that it is a result to be reached only in the "long run." The idea of the long run was a happy hunting ground for Royce, and it caused the pragmatists much trouble. When Peirce speaks of a certain ratio having a certain value in the "long run," he means that an endless succession of fractions has a probability limit, and this is a value, as he says, "about which the values of the endless succession will never cease to oscillate" (2.758). The long run, that is, means an endless series, and only if we have an endless series are we able to ascribe to it a finite character. There is no contradiction, Peirce holds, in the idea of an endless series of finite terms having a finite *sum*. And yet he was willing to admit that the endless succession as such cannot be experienced (see 5.528) "but involves a first dose of ideality, or generality." The entire conception of the long run is not without a certain ambiguity. Sometimes it clearly means the endlessness itself of the series and the denial that any finite number of terms adequately expresses the "would-be." Sometimes it means what was referred to above as the probability limit, in which emphasis falls not on the endlessness of the series but on its convergence to a stable result. Happily we may leave the problem of the actual infinite, which is precisely the problem to which this discussion points, to other papers on Peirce. For our purpose it is sufficient to note that for Peirce the appeal to the long run is to an endless succession required for exhibiting a finite character and to a succession which cannot be experienced as such.

(5) *The mode of real possibility, or the "would-be"* This topic is so central to Peirce's system that it might be used as a basis for unifying the whole. We can be concerned with it only insofar as it figures in the theory of reality. The real has been identified as an ultimate opinion that would be reached under certain circumstances. An opinion expressing the result of inquiry takes conceptual form and, according to Peirce's pragmaticism, conceptual meaning is understood in terms of the way things would behave in the long run. Real possibility, therefore, figures twice over in the definition of reality; on the one hand it concerns the process of inquiry and the opinion that would result if the process were pushed to the limit; on the other hand the "would-be" concerns the nature of an opinion and the proper interpretation of what Peirce called "intellectual purport." We shall consider only the latter.

The nature of a thing means a totality of behavior including all that the thing has done and all that it would do in an endless series of relevant occasions. The "would-be" of a die, for example, could be expressed only in a series of conditional propositions stating the behavior of the die throughout an endless series of relevant events. Peirce compares this to a habit in the case of man. The nature of a man defined through habits means understanding him through real possibilities of behavior. The "would-be" or reality of the man is not identical with the behavior, either in the sense of a given act or a finite collection of them. If we may paraphrase the expression of John Stuart Mill, the "would-be" in Peirce's scheme is a permanent possibility of behavior. The key to the discovery of the "would-be," Peirce says, is what actually happens, but this is only a small part of the totality.[9] The ultimate or stable opinion is supposed to express the "would-be" in its totality. That opinion is not a mere recital of a series of events, but the expression of the habit or the power of the thing to behave in that way. How the "would-be" is a totality Peirce has not explained.

The pragmatistic theory of reality—the defining of the real through inquiry, stable belief, and the "would-be" of real possibility—is supposed to do justice to realism and idealism at the same time. Peirce believed that it was legitimate to take the idealist line and connect reality essentially with thought and opinion as long as the thought involved was independent of the finite and fallible thinker, and as long as it was not conceived in a "mentalistic" way. The interpretation of conceptual meaning in terms of habit and behavior rather than intuited, immediate ideas is intended to satisfy the latter demand, and the community of inquirers following an interpersonal method is supposed to satisfy the former demand. The realism, that is to say, is a realism of the dynamical nature of the object and of objective thought; the idealism is that of a rationalism according to which the real is defined as the result of a process of knowledge. The two elements or emphases find their proper place within a wider matrix of

9. The most important passages for understanding the theory of real possibility are: 1.420; 2.661–68; 4.580; 5.453, 5.467, 5.528; 6.327.

Community and Reality

inquiry, understood, to be sure, in the most concrete of terms, that is, as the controlled process of fixing belief and of moving from doubt and hesitation to belief and confident action.

The question that remains, however, is whether the entire system does not stand or fall with the validity of Peirce's special version of what we may call the "possible experience" doctrine. For it is in the doctrine of real possibility that the realistic and idealistic elements are combined. Realism demands an object that is always "all there," and in no way in need of an idea to represent it; instead Peirce offers a realism of Secondness, objective thought, and the "would-be" of behavior. Idealism demands actual presence of reality to thought or to mind; instead Peirce offers an idealism of eventual belief or stable opinion as the "would-be" of inquiry. It may be that Peirce was right in his reinterpretation of both realism and idealism, but wrong in his belief that a theory of reality can be founded on a theory of possibility, even so subtle a theory as that of the Scotistic realism.

CRITICAL COMMENTS

There are three major difficulties with the theory of reality outlined above. All stem from a common source: the defining of the real through the context of knowledge. Peirce, that is to say, for all of his understanding of the need for an ontological theory, still belonged to that modern tradition in philosophy according to which the key to *being* is found through *being known*. I want to suggest three critical points at which Peirce's theory shows the limitations of that approach. First, there is the problem of saying precisely what sort of reality is enjoyed by an ultimate *opinion* that would be, but in fact is not, apprehended by any finite community of knowers; second, there is the well-known problem of the futurism involved in pragmaticism and in what sense it can allow for *presence* of the total or unified person or thing; third, there is the problem of the reality of the several dimensions of things—esthetic, moral, religious, political—that seem to be excluded when the real is defined through the differential and highly abstract medium of theoretical science.

115

We can best see the point of the first criticism if we turn to Peirce's encounter with Royce. In his reviews of *The World and the Individual* (8.100 ff.), Peirce attempted to meet Royce's charge that reality cannot be identified with an intellectual result or opinion unless that opinion is actual and not merely possible. Royce claimed that possible experience is inadequate for defining the real, and that if we think in terms of reality as a final or critical judgment there must be a mind or form of experience capable of having that judgment as actual experience. Royce, of course, in holding to the reality of the Absolute experience, could define the real object as beyond finite thought by identifying it with the truth about it already possessed by the Absolute knowledge. Thus what the community of investigators *would* arrive at is precisely what the Absolute has as actual experience. In having a point of actual experience beyond finite experience, Royce has a ground for an actual object that is to be known by the finite community but is not dependent on that human knowledge. He has a real object beyond human thought, even if there are problems connected with the Absolute experience. Peirce saw one aspect of the difficulty, and admitted that the object at which the inquirers aim cannot be a future idea or opinion, for if the object of the ultimate opinion is another opinion in the future an infinite progress breaks out, and the result can only be the substitution of an abstraction for the real. Peirce's acknowledgment of the point is clear and unequivocal: "There is no escaping the admission that the ultimate end of inquiry—the essential, not ulterior end—the mould to which we endeavor to shape our opinions, cannot itself be of the nature of an opinion" (8.104). Instead of following out the consequences of this line and questioning the adequacy of identifying the real with an opinion in the first place, Peirce turned instead to dialectical criticism and attacked Royce's claim that the possible experience is no more than a "bare" or "mere" possibility. What makes this polemical comedy of genuine philosophical interest is that Peirce did lay hold of a genuine difficulty in Royce's theory, and indeed Royce later tried to correct it, ironically enough with help from Peirce, by moving away from the Absolute and on to the community of interpretation theory developed in *The Problem of Christianity*. Peirce, on the other hand, went back to a defense of the theory of real possibility armed with the insight—which is true—that Royce failed to appreciate the problem of real possibility, being content, as Peirce acutely said, with no mode of reality poorer than that of actuality.

What we have here is a case of failure to develop one's own theory adequately because of the temptation to correct the mistakes of others. Peirce was right, and Royce later attempted to correct his own omission, but the fact remains that Peirce did not see the consequences of his own admission. If the ultimate aim of inquiry is an object and not an opinion, how can the reality of that object be defined in terms of an opinion that would be found if inquiry were pushed to its ultimate end in the long run? Royce, being a wholehearted idealist, could accept the identification of the real with knowledge because he could always answer the question as to who gets the ultimate insight as an actual possession by appealing either to the Absolute experience or, as in the later philosophy, to the reality of the Cause to which the community of inquirers is dedicated. But Peirce was not a wholehearted idealist, and was even a Scotistic realist to boot: he had no way both of allowing that reality is an opinion or intellectual result and of giving to that opinion more support than it receives from the theory of real possibility. Royce saw that if to have a real object means a process of inquiry then that process must have an actual issue or fulfillment, and if it does not, we are left with an abstraction.

The defenders of Peirce will want at this point to call up the realistic reserves and claim that by the ultimate *opinion* Peirce does not mean a finite thought and he certainly does not mean anything mental. True, the opinion that expresses the total "would-be" of the object must be understood in terms of behavior and of power to continue in the pattern of the habit. Thus it might be said that since the opinion in question is not the sort of reality that needs to be actual in a mind, Royce's charge fails to be conclusive. But even allowing for the most completely non-idealistic interpretation of real possibility and the "would-be," whether you can identify the real with any ultimate state of affairs that is not actual, and can be reached only in the long run, remains a problem. Peirce no doubt believed that, to use the language of James, the "cash value" of the long run can be supplied by the theory of real possibility, but even so it remains true that, on Peirce's own admission, the long run has a large dose of ideality or generality in it. My conclusion is this: pile possibility on possibility, even real possibility on real possibility, and the result is not the real, but the really possible. Reality in the end for Peirce is future experience, and this is not enough.

The second difficulty may be treated shortly since it points to a criticism of the pragmatic approach that has often been made. To identify the real with the future, even the rich and full-bodied future of Peirce's realism, is to lose the totality of an object or a person within *present* experience. It is not necessary to transform the world into a timeless, pure actuality to view it as having an integral unity and totality *at each present moment* in time. I may confront another person and be aware that he is still growing and developing and yet also be aware that, although incomplete, he confronts me as a unity and total self in every present encounter. Another way of putting the point is to say that the other self does not become a real individual unity *only* at the point where the final opinion about him is reached. The fact is that Peirce was well aware of this point, and as we have seen he used the idea of the indexical sign that denotes the real individual at the beginning of inquiry against Royce's claim that only perfect knowledge serves to individuate. But Peirce seems to have overlooked the fact that the present integrity of the real individual is lost if that reality is identified with an opinion or type of experience that never manages to establish itself in the present. The unity and totality of the individual both transcend and are ingredient in every stage of the process of development; they do not wait to be constituted by the limit of a process of experience that can be reached only in the future.[10]

10. I do not overlook the fact that Peirce (see 7.340 ff.) sought to respond to the difficulty cited by claiming that the reality does not *begin* to be the way it is said to be in the idea or belief when the belief first comes into being. He

Community and Reality

My final point concerns the limitation of the standpoint marked out by scientific inquiry. Peirce seems to have underestimated the differential character of the controlled, theoretical inquiry that is to issue in the real truth about things. The question may fairly be raised as to whether the knowing relation is the only relation in which we stand to the world and to the things in it. Ethics, esthetics, and religion point to dimensions of things that are excluded from the highly precise, and therefore abstract, considerations that alone are relevant for scientific inquiry. This is not to say that Peirce neglected these other dimensions in his thought; it is rather to say that they cannot easily be included by a theory of reality in which the ultimate truth comes from scientific inquiry alone. The reality of things is not exhausted in their being material for knowledge. This is the great error of much modern philosophy; Peirce was not free from it.

---

attempts to disconnect the being of the object from the idea, while claiming that the only *meaning* we can give to the descriptive term or idea is by pointing to the actual behavior.

Chapter 5   Charles S. Peirce, Philosopher

Paul Weiss

I   Peirce had size. His was an unusually fine and honest mind, sustained by a burning passion for learning and a lifelong devotion to philosophy. He combined strong analytic powers with an interest in system, and backed them with great pertinacity enlivened with flashes of decided originality. These splendid gifts enabled him to make signal and lasting contributions in many areas.

He who is without a good mind will not often see beyond the surface of things, nor will he see very far. And when he does see something, he will lack the concepts and the power to grasp what it means or how it is related to what else is known. If that mind be not radically honest as well, more likely than not it will falter before the really hard questions. Long established, popular doctrines will go unchallenged; limitations will be ignored or blurred. The more daring judgments will be qualified, hobbled, and perhaps hidden or disguised.

Without a burning passion for learning, a man will tend to do little more than repeat what he has heard, or what he has already accepted from others. All of us are hemmed in by the long entrenched, the accepted, and the inherited, and thereby kept from tackling what is rejected or unknown. Only a genuine passion to know will help one burn a way through what otherwise would keep us prisoners to the little we already know.

Despite a lifetime of neglect by philosophers, publishers, administrators, and other influential contemporaries, despite financial difficulties and poor health, Peirce worked year in and year out on his philosophy. His was a devotion of some fifty years. No one without his sincere desire to find things out, sustained over the decades, can have much hope of making a signal contribution to philosophy. The tissue of philosophic thought is so delicate, the problems it deals with are so overrun with misconceptions, preconceptions, prejudices, and confusions, that there is no one who is at times not lost, disoriented, and perhaps disheartened. The scholar's life is a lonely one, but the philosopher's life is lonelier still. He looks critically even at what he himself cherishes. The prevailing doctrines, the dominant religions, the current myths, the reigning fashions of thought—no one is sacrosanct. He approaches all in the same spirit of sympathetic detachment, subjecting their grounds and their claims to a searching, probing examination. He lives for the most part in an unmapped world, sustained by an unquenchable desire to make it intelligible.

A man might have a good and honest mind, and give himself wholeheartedly to the pursuit of knowledge. Yet the outcome might be little more than blunders, distortions, vague generalizations. Nothing less than strong analytic powers will protect one from such a dismal prospect. They will help us find the joints where what we confront can be properly divided, relate distant items in the light of their mutual relevance, master the appearances, cut beneath the obtrusive aspect of things to find the solid base on which they rest. It is one of the glories of our time that most of the "professional" philosophers today have considerable analytic ability, though I think few are as strong as Peirce. Fewer still are as wide-ranging or as bold. But even these fail to balance and structure their analytic studies by an interest in system, directed at grasping the whole of things and knowledge.

We live in a world where there are many somewhat independent pockets of affiliated items. We find ourselves among many types of entities: things, animals, and men; secular, sacramental, art, and artifactual objects; created, lived-in, and physical space; musical, historic, and natural time. We are helped by dedicated workers in many specialized disciplines, each in its own way pushing back the borders of ignorance. How these different entities and disciplines clarify, support, and are related to one another, how they fit within the purview of a single account, is a matter of considerable importance and should be a question of great philosophic interest. No one can hope to make much progress in understanding even a fragment of all there is and can be known who does not have some idea of the whole to which it belongs. A philosopher worthy of the name has an encompassing view, vague and ultimately unsatisfactory though it may prove to be. Unsupported by analysis it will soon turn out to be little more than an untidy, warm, felt unity. But without such a view, the most thorough analysis can yield little more than tiresome details supported by assumptions unexamined and perhaps indefensible.

Peirce was a most persistent man. He returned again and again enthusiastically and vigorously to the same questions and problems, constantly refining, reorganizing, and rethinking them. The result would have been monotonous were it not for his striking originality, breaking through the characteristic conventional views of his time, place, and culture.

His were great virtues, almost sufficient to define him as a great mind. Peirce backed them by a vast erudition and a solid grounding in laboratory work. His knowledge of the history of logic was second to none, and his knowledge of the history of science and the history of philosophy were almost as large and as sure. Because he is one of the very few students in the philosophy of science who actually engaged in serious laboratory work, demanding precision and care, he is one of the very few who speak with authority, and persuasively. Too much of current work in the philosophy of science seems to be the outcome of reflections on popular accounts of great scientific work. How refreshing it is to turn to Peirce. Though he wrote before the days of relativity and quanta, what he has to say about the spirit and method of science rings clear and true, and seems to be as luminous as anything said today.

Peirce has still to receive all the recognition that he deserves. We find him referred to primarily as the founder of pragmatism, though this was only a fragment of a much larger view, which held that doubt is an unwanted and undesirable goad, an involuntary state of affairs from which we seek to escape through reasoning, ending in a settled belief expressed in purposive action.

Charles S. Peirce, Philosopher

"Doubt is an uneasy and dissatisfied state from which we struggle to free ourselves and pass into the state of belief; while the latter is a calm and satisfactory state which we do not wish to avoid, or to change to a belief in anything else" (5.372; see also 5.373 ff., 5.563). "The elements of every concept . . . make their exit at the gate of purposive action" (5.212; see also 2.173). He refused to ontologize his pragmatism, "pragmatism is, in itself, no doctrine of metaphysics, no attempt to determine any truth of things. It is merely a method" (5.464; see also 5.13 n., 5.14, 5.18), and he refused to exaggerate its importance (5.18; see also 5.14). Peirce deserves much credit for his initial formulation of the doctrine and his many reformulations of it. But he deserves at least as much credit for his refusal to allow it to swallow up his other interests and his other pursuits.

Peirce did not publish much on pragmatism, and what he published was largely for the sake of differentiating his view from the more popular accounts of James and Schiller. (See particularly 5.414.) Most of Peirce's respected work was in technical logic, now published in volumes 3 and 4 of the *Collected Papers*. His contributions to that subject have now for the most part been already absorbed in the rapidly moving stream of logical studies. What still endures in its own right is his philosophy of logic, with its classification and analysis of different types of reasoning. Most of that material is in volume 2. Logic for him was concerned with understanding the nature of controlled thinking, a thinking carried out on behalf of a community of inquirers. "Reasoning is essentially a voluntary act, over which we exercise control" (2.144; see also 2.200, 2.1); ". . . logicality inexorably requires that our interests shall *not* be limited . . . It must reach . . . beyond all bounds . . . Logic is rooted in the social principle" (2.654; see also 5.354). It was not mathematical in spirit or intent. "The business of drawing demonstrative conclusions from assumed premises . . . is the sole business of the mathematician . . . The business of logic [is] analysis and theory of reasoning, but not the practice of it" (4.134; see also 4.228, 4.229). Mathematics did, logic understood.

Not much in Peirce's account of deduction is genuinely new or important, though I think it is most helpful to distinguish with him premises from leading principles, and leading principles from logical principles. Premises are antecedents, leading principles are rules governing the passage from those antecedents to their consequences, while logical principles are those leading principles which add no content to an argument, but which can be abstracted from every movement from premiss to conclusion. Logical principles are therefore to be found in every bit of reasoning, making logic a subject pertinent to every discipline and rational enterprise (2.462–66). No inference, deductive or otherwise, is to be understood in isolation. Each must be seen to be a critical, controlled activity, one instance of a class of similar activities. "A person who draws a rational conclusion, not only thinks it to be true, but thinks that similar reasoning would be just in every analogous case. If he fails to think this, the inference is not to be called reasoning" (1.606; see also 2.444).

His account of induction, though not as detailed as that of deduction, is more striking and original. It was for him a self-corrective agency (2.729) which if persisted in would arrive at or approximate the final truth. *"Induction* is that mode of reasoning which adopts a conclusion as approximate, because it results from a method of inference which must generally lead to the truth in the long run" (1.67; see also 2.269). On the basis of fair sampling, induction determines the value of a given hypothesis. The business of induction "consists in testing a hypothesis" (2.755). "All that induction can do is to ascertain the value of a ratio" (1.67; see also 2.269). One need not share in Peirce's firm belief in the inevitable achievement of final truth in order to be able to treat induction, with him, as a self-corrective means for reaching a better understanding of what we had originally supposed.

Peirce's most outstanding contribution in logic was his theory of abduction, the means by which we get new ideas. He left no systematic treatise on the subject, but out of his various references to it one can, I think, point to a more systematic account. This I once tried to do.[1] A quotation from that previous study may,

1. "The Logic of the Creative Process," *Studies in the Philosophy of Charles Sanders Peirce,* ed. P. P. Wiener and F. H. Young (Cambridge, Mass., 1952), pp. 166–82.

Charles S. Peirce, Philosopher

for the present purposes, suffice to show the importance abduction had for him. He saw that it was "of the very essence of pragmatism, saw that it was essential to history, and that it constituted the first stage of all inquiries. He insisted that it was a necessary part of perception, memory, and science. He thought it had a bearing on a proof of God, and that it was presupposed by all induction"[2] (5.196, 6.606 n., 2.714, 6.469, 4.541, 5.181, 2.625, 5.172, 6.458 ff., 2.755 f.). Much work needs to be done in this area. It is regrettable that logicians are not yet ready to follow Peirce into this most promising field.

Long before the days of quanta Peirce rejected the doctrines of simple mechanism and determinism. "Mechanical law can never produce diversification" (1.174). "I believe I have thus subjected to fair examination all the important reasons for adhering to the theory of universal necessity, and have shown their nullity" (6.65). He came to this position in part because he tried to understand why there are different kinds of things apparently distributed at random throughout space, in part because he took evolution to be a cosmic force, and in part because he sought an explanation for the occurrence of both laws and minds, compulsions and purposes. Determinism and mechanism take variety to be given and inexplicable. Nor can they account for growth and novelty. Recourse must be had to a genuine spontaneity, to Chance, a fresh, expansive, originative source of unpredictable diversity.[3]

Among his many permanent contributions to knowledge one must count his single-handed development of a rather complete science of signs.[4] As time went on he became more and more enamored with the idea that everything whatsoever was a sign. "The entire phenomenal manifestation of mind, is a sign" (5.313). "The word or sign which man uses *is* the man himself" (5.314). "A human being . . . being a sign himself" (6.344). The world of signs in fact formed a single whole, in which sign referred to sign and was interpreted by another sign, and so on apparently without end (2.92). Over the years his account became more and

2. Ibid., p. 166.
3. *Collected Papers, 6*, Bk. 1, Ch. 2, "The Doctrine of Necessity Examined."
4. Ibid., 2, Bk. 2, Chs. 2, 3.

more complex (8.344 ff.).[5] Few of his distinctions seem to have been put to much use. Yet in the course of that development he makes many arresting points, of which only a few have been noted by subsequent thinkers, and these not at the center of his thought. He recognized that nouns depend on pronouns and not the other way around: "a noun is an imperfect substitute for a pronoun" (2.287 n.). He knew that terms are incomplete propositions, and propositions incomplete arguments: "That which remains of a Proposition after removal of its Subject is a Term (a rhema). . . . That which remains of an Argument when its Conclusion is removed is a Proposition" (2.95); and he makes unmistakably evident how indices differ from symbols, and propositional functions from propositions (2.248, 2.249, 2.250, 2.251).

Less well-known, though of considerable importance, are Peirce's studies in methodology, his account of natural classes, his defense of Scotistic realism, his Critical Common-sensism, his phenomenology, and his acknowledgment of the indeterminate and the vague. Brief comments on each of these I think are in order.

Peirce was always interested in methods (2.110). He took logic itself to be a method for classifying and evaluating ways of discovering the truth (3.364, 3.454). Pragmatism too was a method. ". . . *pragmatism* is not a *Weltanschauung* but is a method of reflexion having for its purpose to render ideas clear" (5.13 n.; see also 5.464, 5.467). He sometimes referred to his doctrines of chance and continuity as essentially methodological agencies (6.606). Even what he called metaphysics was rooted in his acceptance of the Kantian method of metaphysical deduction, whereby logical distinctions are converted into basic ways of organizing experiential data (3.454, 2.121, 1.300, 1.374). The great problem of the day for him was that of discovering methods. "One of the main problems of logic [is] that of producing a method for the discovery of methods in mathematics" (3.364; see also 3.454).

For the modern logician, a class is a mere aggregate. Bring any entities, no matter how alien or heterogeneous, together, and you

5. See also Paul Weiss and Arthur Burks, "Peirce's Sixty-Six Signs," *Journal of Philosophy, 42* (1945), 383–88.

then, according to them, will have formed a class. For the Marxist a class is more than an aggregate. It forcefully relates a number of men through common interests and for a common destiny. Peirce stood between these two extremes. With the modern logicians he knew that there were classes of entities other than men (1.205); with the Marxists he could see that some classes were defined by governing principles (1.204). He has, I think, something to teach both schools. Interested in classifying the sciences on a rational basis,[6] convinced that ideas govern their instances—"every lamp has been made and has come into being as a result of an aim common and peculiar to all lamps" (1.204)—willing to accept the reality of final causation—" 'natural', or 'real', class . . . a class the existence of whose members is due to a common and peculiar final cause" (1.211)—he was able to show how at least artifactual objects were to be grouped. It is to be noted that for Peirce a final cause is not an efficient cause working backwards in time, but one where the unity or whole governs and perhaps produces the subordinate elements. "Efficient causation is that kind of causation whereby the parts compose the whole; final causation is that kind of causation whereby the whole calls out its parts" (1.220).

Throughout his life Peirce was a realist—but not a Platonist. He denied that universals had a reality of their own, standing off by themselves (1.27 n.). What he insisted on was that words (2.292) and other universals (1.27, 8.14) are not only indeterminate (1.434) but efficacious (1.217), able to relate, govern, and call for the particularities that they ruled. There were genuine "would-be's" in things; "to say that a die has a 'would-be' is to say that it has a property, quite analogous to any *habit* that a man might have" (2.664; see also 2.665; 5.105). He who denied this was a nominalist, unable to account for the effectiveness of ideas, purposes, and science (1.20, 1.422; 5.107, 5.312, 5.423; 6.588).

Peirce's realism is closely tied up with his understanding of the laws of nature. A law of nature is how an endless future must come to be (5.545). Operative in what does take place, a law of nature does not make it take place—"no law of nature makes a stone fall"

---

6. *Collected Papers, 1,* Bk. 2.

(1.323). The laws evolve and must therefore be understood in the light of the operation of Chance or spontaneity. "Now the only possible way of accounting for the laws of nature and for uniformity in general is to suppose them results of evolution. This supposes them not to be absolute, not to be obeyed precisely. It makes an element of . . . absolute chance in nature" (6.13; see also 1.174).

In recent years there has been a revival of the originally Scotch view that the everyday world is at once ultimate and real. The dominant versions today are German, French, and English. Differing in many basic respects, they all agree that the stabilized outlook of commonplace men has an irreducible being or meaning. Peirce's Critical Common-sensism[7] both accords and disaccords with essential features of this position. He thought that, on the whole, unreflecting common sense was close to the core of reality and truth. But he refused to say that there were truly fixed items in the common sense world which were forever beyond all criticism. "Our instinctive beliefs, in their original condition, are so mixed up with error that they can never be trusted till they have been corrected by experiment" (1.404). Neither in the common-sense world nor elsewhere would he grant that there were infallible principles or truths infallibly known. "Indeed, out of a contrite fallibilism, combined with a high faith in the reality of knowledge, and an intense desire to find things out, all my philosophy has always seemed to me to grow" (1.14; see also 1.401, 1.171)—unless it be those which relate to matters of vital importance and have the backing of instinctive and hallowed practice. "Matters of vital importance must be left . . . to instinct" (1.637), ". . . instinct with its almost unerring certainty" (1.496; see also 7.108).

Undoubtedly influenced by the example Hegel set in his *Phenomenology of Mind,* Peirce and Husserl independently and at about the same time developed distinctively different phenomenologies. The Husserlian version is concerned with a description of encountered phenomena, freed from their involvement in the world. Later in life Husserl seemed to affirm that his discoveries had some bearing on the interests of men. But for Peirce phe-

7. Ibid., 5, Bk. 3, Chs. 2, 3.

nomenology is an observational study of basic categorial distinctions present to everyone every minute of the day. It offers a "description . . . of all that is in any way or in any sense present to the mind, quite regardless of whether it corresponds to any real thing or not" (1.284). He took it to be primarily occupied with the isolation of indecomposable elements: a felt monad, an interactive dyad, and a rational triad (1.294, 1.303, 1.305, 1.325, 1.326, 1.337, 1.343, 1.345). He has many illuminating things to say about all three, but none of it is dealt with in the light of man's anxieties, concerns, or being. Peirce remained detached, dispassionate, logical even in his phenomenological investigations.

Peirce's strong antinominalistic and antideterministic attitudes have already been touched upon. He was also strongly opposed to the atomistic doctrine that the world is made up of disconnected particulars. "I like to call my theory Synechism, because it rests on the study of continuity" (6.202). He insisted on the reality of the vague, where oppositional elements merged together: twilight is a good instance, being at once dark and light. He insisted also on the reality of the indeterminate or general where there was a violation of the law of excluded middle, since we are not there forced to choose one of a pair of exclusive alternatives. Man in general is indeterminate, being neither male nor female. "Anything is *general* in so far as the principle of excluded middle does not apply to it and is *vague* in so far as the principle of contradiction does not apply to it" (5.448; see also 5.546, 5.505). His recognition of the presence of the vague and indeterminate enabled Peirce to do justice to the blurred borders of experience as well as to the nature of universals, laws, purposes, and concepts. It enabled him too to give a pragmatic interpretation to the meaning of logical quantifiers (2.453, 5.505). It should have brought him to develop a multivalued logic. But into that land of promise he never entered.

II   These signal, and by no means Peirce's only achievements, are great enough to win a place for him forever in the history of American and nineteenth-century thought. But he has not, and I think he cannot have, a leading place in the history of philosophy itself. Too much of his work is scarred and flawed by his limited philosophic method, his concept of the role of philosophy, by failures in insight, by exaggerations, distortions, dogmatisms, and a distressing streak of inconsistency.

Peirce had singularly little dialectical ability. Rarely did he try to see what things looked like hind-way to. He did not seem ever to consider the possibility that what he took to be first might be viewed as last, and conversely; or that if A (say, experience) were used to test B (say, a theory), B might also provide a test for A. And though he wished to produce a system of philosophy so comprehensive and solidly based that every part of knowledge and being would eventually find a place within it (1.1, 1.176 f.), he in fact contented himself with making swift inductions from experience and generalizing the views of evolutionary biology (6.33, 6.531, 6.6) and theoretical physics (1.7). He expressed little interest in such ontological questions as the nature of Being, Becoming, or Passing Away, the flow of time or the nature of the past. He thought in fact that the problem of whether or not there was a linearly arranged maximum multitude was a more pressing metaphysical question (6.326 n.). In his early period he speculated about the origin of the universe, but within the crippling framework of ideas derived from biology. Too much of his time was spent in classifying, ordering, categorizing material; too much time was spent in refining and rewriting where a re-examination was needed. No thought seems to have been given to the question whether or not philosophy has its own distinctive subject matter, tests, and value (1.126 ff.).

Peirce saw clearly and well the spirit that animates scientific inquirers at their best. He knew them to be imbued with a desire to learn. "For it is not knowing, but the love of learning, that characterizes the scientific man" (1.44; see also 1.235). He knew too that they rejected inexplicables: ". . . to suppose a thing inexplicable is not only to fail to explain it . . . but, much worse, it is to set up a barrier across the road of science" (6.171; see also 1.139). Scientists, ideally viewed, were cooperative (1.99) and unconcerned with utility or popularity. It is "diligent inquiry into truth for truth's sake" (1.44). "True science is distinctively the study of use-

Charles S. Peirce, Philosopher

less things" (1.76; see also 1.670). He wanted philosophy and other disciplines to exhibit that same spirit (1.663, 1.644, 1.235, 1.236). How heartening it would be were more men to heed that challenging call! But Peirce was not content to have men capture the spirit of scientific inquirers. Dominated by the view that science offered a perfect model of inquiry (5.385 ff.), he wanted to extend its method to all others (7.60 ff.). Philosophy itself should become scientific. "Philosophy ought to imitate the successful sciences in its methods" (5.265). "I wish philosophy to be a strict science" (5.537). It should become severely technical. "The philosophy of the future must, like the other sciences, be put forth chiefly in the form of memoirs" written with an "immense technical vocabulary" and without literary style (8.169). Though many moderns would applaud this program, nothing, I think, could be more disastrous for the future of thought. Philosophy is not and ought not to aspire to be a science. It is one of the humanities. Instead of being engaged in piecemeal investigations carried on within the framework of accepted but unexamined presuppositions, it relentlessly probes to the foundations of thought and being. It seeks to know what all inquiries presuppose, what all of them cherish, what all of them need. We must look to it if we are to learn what is at the root of man's being, what being itself is, the nature of change and fixity, the real and the valuable, what obligation is, and what kinds of necessity there be. Where else can we find systematic inquiries into the foundations of society and state, the nature of art, history, religion, and education? Where else will these be dealt with from the perspective of tested broad principles, purified by criticism and checked by experience?

The closest Peirce came to acknowledging a distinctive philosophic method was in his phenomenological studies, his classification of signs, and his adoption of the Kantian metaphysical deduction of the categories. Peirce was one of the very few students of Kant who thought that this method of discovering the basic categories of being or knowledge had much promise. "A metaphysics not founded on the science of logic is of all branches of scientific inquiry the most shaky and insecure" (2.36; see also 1.561, 1.625, 3.454). Such a view helped him to look for his Firsts and Seconds in unsuspected areas, but I think this was but a small gain for a failure to use more flexible, more wide-ranging, better grounded ultimate principles. Is it true that philosophy must treat logical principles as truths of being (1.487)? And if it is true, which of the multitude of logical distinctions, constants, formulae, and classifications are to be used as our guides?

Quite early in his career Peirce came to the conclusion that he had to acknowledge just three categories.[8] Initially they seemed to function for him as factual finders, but too soon they came to be treated as constitutive. They were reified, almost deified. He saw instances and illustrations of them everywhere—in reasoning, metaphysics, psychology, physiology, biology, physics.[9] It led him to invent some new sciences, e.g. chemology, psychognosy (1.260, 1.267), and to treat feeling, freedom, immediacy, the admirable under a single head; duality, struggle, brute existence, will, indices, exclamations under a second; and thought, mind, purposes, continuity, and interpretants under a third.[10] Still, it was through their agency that he was able to build up his theory of signs, carry out his classification of the sciences and arguments, and to come to see that he had neglected the study of esthetics and ethics. But these gains were, as I think will become more evident, over-balanced by the serious losses they entailed.

All knowledge, Peirce thought, comes from observation (2.444). The doctrine seems most implausible. But implausible or not, it points up the fact that he himself seemed to be a poor observer. This is a conclusion to which one comes most reluctantly, because he insisted again and again that he was a most careful observer, a most disciplined and conscientious patient discriminator of sensations of all sorts (7.44, 7.256, 7.396). To question the role of observation in his view would be to deny some of his most important theses. He maintained constantly that such disciplines as mathematics (1.240), logic (1.238), and of course phenomenology were observational sciences. He went so far at times as to maintain that a reasoner had to make use of diagrams. "All necessary reasoning

8. Ibid., *1*, Bk. 3, Ch. 6.
9. Ibid., Ch. 3.
10. Ibid., Bk. 3 passim.

without exception is diagrammatic" (5.162; see also 1.66, 2.267, 8.118), never questioning the fact that a diagram is displayed in a three-dimensional Euclidean space and therefore must distort the nature of whatever does not fit into such a space. More important, though, is what he reports about his Firsts, Seconds, and Thirds. Little of it can, I think, withstand critical scrutiny.

Firstness is immediacy (1.328, 6.18), simple (6.345), indeterminate (6.13, 6.206), perhaps vague (6.186), without affiliations or resemblances (1.310). He held that it had no unity (1.357), and that every description falsified it (5.49). But surely it has endless nuances, and is always highly complex. A single sound has countless overtones, increasing and decreasing intensities; it reverberates, echoes, and re-echoes. A patch of color varies in light and shadow throughout; it has swellings and depressions; here it rushes forward and there it retreats. The feeling of pain, the smell of cabbage are abrasive, disruptive, overwhelming, expanding and contracting, with powers and values, thin in one place, thick in another. Peirce himself sometimes saw that what he called a true First was nowhere to be found in experience (1.304). He is right here, I think, but the admission is, I also think, difficult for one who wants to make phenomenology an observational study. Nor can I confidently always distinguish his Firstness from his Thirdness. Both are at times viewed as indeterminate, continuous, normative, and productive of whatever there is. That he thinks one is irrational and the other rational is quite evident, but why he thinks so is very hard to see.

Peirce clearly saw that one of Hegel's great weaknesses was his neglect of particularity, of the *hic et nunc* of experience, of struggle and brutality, of insistence and resistance, the vital interchange we encounter everywhere and all the time. "The capital error of Hegel which permeates the whole system in every part of it is that he almost altogether ignores the Outward Clash" (8.41; see also 1.368, 5.79, 5.91). Without indices, denotatives, pronouns which made contact with the objects in the world, no statement, Peirce knew, could be more than a generality, having no necessary application to any matter of fact. "No matter of fact can be stated without the use of some sign serving as an index" (2.305; see also

2.287 n.). But Peirce did not want to go behind phenomena, leave the obtrusively present (5.452, 5.525, 5.553). As a consequence his Secondness came to express only a facet, only a dimension of experience. It does not pull him outside the realm of feeling and thought to put him in touch with real substantial exterior objects (1.324, 1.332). Like every other Hegelian he was confined within the orbit of his cognized and felt content. To be sure, he insisted that the world was not his own creation (6.95). There were realities which were independent of anyone's idea of them, the termini at which inquiry will eventually arrive (5.384). But this is not yet to say that we can move below the surface of things. Yet do we not do so in perception and in action, when making something, in sympathy, and in love? Is it not more correct to say that we encounter *objects* that resist rather than that we meet with resistance or find our volitional inertia challenged (1.332)? Resistance would be a brute antirational component in experience, as Peirce took it to be, were it not part of an encounter with another being.

There could, thought Peirce, be Firsts and Seconds without Thirds (5.90 ff.). So far as he held such a view he was more Kantian than Hegelian. But the general trend of his thought was toward idealism, in which Thirdness or rationality was the primary fact, and the absolute—or totality—and ultimately real was the body of settled opinion accepted by an unlimited community of inquirers. "The one intelligible theory of the universe is that of objective idealism, that matter is effete mind, inveterate habits becoming physical laws" (6.25; see also 6.102). With other idealists he held that there were no realities independent of thought. "It is quite beyond the power of mind to have an idea of something entirely independent of thought" (7.345; see also 7.361). He said there were no individuals (3.93, 3.216, 5.448 n.), and that all of us are but elements in a larger whole. "Now you and I—what are we? Mere cells of the social organism . . . there is nothing which distinguishes my personal identity except my faults and my limitations . . . my blind will, which it is my highest endeavor to annihilate" (1.673). Even space and time for him were generals (5.530, 6.96). Everything that is thought to exist in the final opinion is real and nothing else (8.12, 8.16, 5.311). But are not

Charles S. Peirce, Philosopher

Thirds structures, arrangements, organizations which, though effective, are not dominant? Are they really thoughts? Are they not, instead, what thought must try to comprehend? And are they not but parts of more substantial beings which crowd out room for themselves in this spatio-temporal dynamic world of distinctive intelligible realities?

Though his account in the end comes down to the adoption of an idealism, freed from all dialectic and put at the service of logic and scientific inquiry, he himself leaned toward the use of dualistic distinctions. Again and again he contrasts the intellectual and the moral, the reasoned and the instinctive, the interior and the exterior, the inner and the outer, mind and matter. Toward the end of his career he spoke of these extremes as differing only in degree,[11] but it is hard to see how this is possible if they are governed by distinctive types of causation.

A man without students, given to the pursuit of difficult thought every day of his life, but denied the benefit of conversation and criticism, tends to be strident at times. Still, one remains disturbed by some of Peirce's exaggerations and dogmatic assertions. His realism became almost an obsession with him. Nominalism was everywhere; even Scotus who, for him, was the greatest of realists, was said to be tinged with nominalism (1.560; 1.19). Sometimes he forgot his great injunction that we ought not to block the road to inquiry (1.135) and held that some ideas are too revolting to be believed. He said that he who occupies himself with the problem of evil is engaged in the blasphemous attempt to define God's purpose (8.263). His attitude toward criminals was at once naïve and cruel (2.164). In the teeth of an almost universal rejection he continued to maintain the view that there were real infinitesimals (4.151, 4.152, 4.664, 3.563 ff.). He even thought they were present in space and time; the present moment, for example, he held to be immeasurably small (5.462, 6.126, 6.132). But then even continuity for him presupposes infinitesimals (1.166).

At times Peirce could be almost petulantly dogmatic. We should, he said, pitch overboard any metaphysics that preaches against

11. Ibid., 6, Bk. 1, Ch. 6.

his three categories (4.318). He thought that we should "adopt Monism as a provisional hypothesis . . . whether we think it likely or not" (6.73). He held that reason did not explain anything except on a theistic hypothesis (6.613), that everything which will be thought to exist in the final opinion is right and nothing else (8.12), and that the more natural and anthropomorphic an idea the more likely it is to be true (5.47). Some justification can be found for most of these, but he was content to let them stand with little defense or excuse.

More understandable, given the climate of the day, but still un-palatable, is his radical acceptance of the theory of evolution, which drove him to envisage an initial state of absolute indeter-minacy or nullity and a gradual rigidification or habituation of the course of affairs until all was hidebound with habits (6.33, 6.196, 6.198, 6.217, 6.220, 1.409). Then there would be a complete reign of law, no mind but only matter (6.25, 6.102).

Dominated by the idea of a hierarchy, he came to acknowledge five pre-logical sciences which had no need of the controlled reason-ing of logic (2.197, 1.183 f.), and took both physics and psychology to be dependent on philosophy for their principles (1.249 ff.). He thought that because reasoning is a species of controlled conduct it must depend on ethics (1.611, 2.582, 5.419), the subject that occupies itself with controlled conduct. And since ethics presup-poses that there is an ultimate aim (1.611, 1.612), he thought that it must depend on esthetics, the subject concerned with making evident what is admirable in itself.

Everywhere the main fact for him was growth (6.58). Even death and corruption were thought to be only accidents or secondary phenomena (6.490). Despite this concern for the vital movement of things in time, he had little feeling for the nature or course of history. He thought the historian was primarily occupied with making conjectures (7.189, 1.511); indeed, history for him was dependent on physics (1.255). And just as Dewey and Mead later found themselves in considerable difficulty when dealing with the past, he also seemed baffled by its reality. All he could deal with were assertions about it, and then as referring to the future. "The fact that Napoleon did ruin his marvellous career *consists* in the fact that anybody who looks for them will find a thousand and one vestiges of that career" (8.194; see also 5.565).

His pragmatism led him into other untenable positions. It prompted him to say that questions which had no practical bearings were meaningless. "As for questions which have no conceivable practical bearings, as the question whether force is an entity, they mean nothing and may be answered as we like, without error" (8.43). He held that what cannot be doubted cannot be criticized (2.144), and that no one could or ought to doubt voluntarily (2.26, 5.261, 5.443); that all conclusions must refer to the future (5.461, 5.539, 5.546); that when doubt ceases, no matter how, the end of reasoning is obtained (7.324); and that the only purpose of inquiry is the settlement of opinion (5.375, 7.327, 7.334, 7.336 n.). He did not pause when his pragmatism made him say that since there was no practical difference that followed on the truth or falsehood of the real presence in the Eucharist, there was nothing for the Protestants and the Roman Catholics to argue about here (5.401). He had trouble giving a pragmatic account of incommensurables and finally concluded that they relate "to what is expectable for a person dealing with fractions" (5.541), as though every idea, the wildest and the most transcendental, could not be treated in this way.

The main drive of Peirce's thought was toward clarification, rationality, understanding. He not only did not want to block the road to inquiry, he not only sought tirelessly to study the methods by which knowledge is achieved, but he maintained that an absolute incognizable existent is a nonsensical phrase (6.419). To find these firm and heartening assertions contradicted again and again is to be first surprised, then disturbed, and finally dismayed. Again and again, for no discernible reason, Peirce says that this, that, and the next thing is unintelligible, unknowable, though indubitably real and ultimate. All Firsts are nonrational and cannot be known (7.465, 5.49). All Seconds are antirational, beyond the reach of generalization. Nor can any percepts be known (5.54, 5.115, 5.568). The truly admirable is so without any reason

(1.612). At times he denigrates reason altogether and applauds instinct instead (1.627), going so far as to claim that animals *never* fall into vital error (1.649), and that the dictates of conscience are practically infallible (1.248). He thinks that there is an instinct for morality but none for rationality (2.160, 2.172 ff., 2.181), and that it is of the essence of the logic of freedom to annul itself (6.219). At one time he asserts that nothing in which we put our trust is absolutely reliable (2.653), though it had been one of his main contentions that the truth is the settled at which we inexorably arrive.

III   These flaws would seriously compromise any philosophy. Were it not for the fact that they are compensated by flashes of insight which point to truths greater than those he had been inclined to defend, Peirce's life work would be little more than a series of interesting and often successful forays in a number of neglected areas. Despite himself, though, almost to his own astonishment, he broke through the limitations of his own method and categories to make evident something of the richness and complexity of knowledge and the world.

There are thinkers who dismiss subjects because they cannot deal with them in terms of their accepted techniques. Peirce was tempted to do this a number of times. But he also acknowledged disciplines for which he had no adequate preparation. One of these was ethics. Though he did little in the field beyond remarking on the soundness of man's judgments in matters of vital importance which precede and outlast man's intellectual formulations,[12] and beyond insisting that ethical considerations were pertinent to logic, leading one to treat all reasoning as involving a reference to an unlimited community of honest inquirers (1.611, 5.354), he did see that it was a normative discipline and dealt with what was in fact good and bad (1.573).

Still later, and then apparently because of the demands of his categorial scheme, he came to recognize the realm of the esthetic.

12. Ibid., *1*, Bk. 4, Ch. 5.

Charles S. Peirce, Philosopher

This he took to be presupposed by ethics and logic, and therefore by everything they hierarchically governed (1.611, 1.612). Though his account of Firsts precluded the esthetic from governing anything, he rightly took it also to be a normative discipline (1.574).

Peirce was alert to the possibility of a continuum of feeling; qualities, he recognized, merge one into the other (1.418, 6.132 ff.). He clearly affirmed that the end of man is not action but the promotion of what he called concrete reasonableness (5.3). He granted that there might be other categories and concepts which are not covered by his. "I by no means deny that there are other categories. On the contrary, at every step of every analysis, conceptions are met with which presumably do not belong to this series of ideas" (1.525). Unfortunately, he does not tell us what these conceptions are. And despite all he had to say about the involuntary character of doubt, he rightly affirms that a metaphysician should be an accomplished doubter (1.624).

Most important, suddenly and somewhat belatedly he came to see that his account of the nature of things was incomplete. In a most perceptive and somewhat surprising paper Peirce acknowledges the reality of God, a being outside of and the source of his categories or universes (6.455 f.). He received many favorable comments on this paper, but apart from Charles Hartshorne's[13] and John E. Smith's studies[14] it has been rather neglected. Yet his pragmatism, phenomenology, and scientism are seriously challenged by this new view. Had Peirce come earlier to the discovery that his three-ply world was incomplete, it would have led him ineluctably to alter some of his basic ideas, and for the better. As it now is, they remain suggestions hovering on the border of what could have been a sound and solid scheme encompassing whatever there be and can be known.

IV   I have learned more from Peirce than from anyone else. Apparently there is no better way for a young man to begin the hazardous lifelong task of becoming a philosopher than by a care-

13. *Philosophical Review, 50* (1941), 516–23.
14. *Studies in the Philosophy of Charles Sanders Peirce,* pp. 251–67.

ful reading of the works of a thoughtful, original, honest, and clear-headed man. The nobility of his spirit in the face of neglect has been for me an inspiration and a challenge. I long ago vowed that I would try not to be a part of a similar miscarriage of justice in my own time. One consequence of this has been the *Review of Metaphysics;* another, the Metaphysical Society of America. Peirce is their spiritual godfather.

Index

Index

Peirce favors Lamarckian, 27; and self-control, 37; as a cosmic force, 125; of laws, 128. *See also* Agapism

Evolutionary: universe, 7, 105; love, 40, 111; metaphysics, 111; biology, 130

Existence, 73, 74, 90. *See also* Secondness

Existentialism, 68, 69, 74, 75, 87

Experience, 72–81, 107, 126, 129 f.; and categories, 69, 70; and Firstness, 72, 73, 133; future, 99, 118; and reality, 101; is a middle term from doubt to belief, 105; ideas tested in the stream of, 109; "possible experience doctrine," 115 f.; and Secondness, 72–75, 134

Experience and Prediction, 45. *See also* Reichenbach

Faith, 16, 21, 24, 26, 31, 36

Fallible: all knowledge essentially, 72, 103; every cognition is, 108

Fallibilism, 32 f., 128

Fay, H. M., 9, 10, 90

Feigl, H., 45, 46, 50

Fermat, P. D., 19

Feuerbach, L., 68

Firstness, 69, 71, 72, 76, 100, 131, 133, 137, 139. *See also* Monad; Quality; Secondness; Thirdness

Fisher, G. P., 3

Fiske, J., 3, 6

Freedom, 16, 17, 132, 138

French philosophy, 19, 67, 128

Froissy, J., 10, 11

Galileo, 64

Gauss, C. F., 53

German, 15, 16, 35, 67, 128. *See also* Philosophy

God, 30, 33, 36, 90, 125, 135, 139

Green, N., 6

Habit, 16, 39, 81, 105, 111; and Thirdness, 75–80, 100 n.; and conduct, 77, and meaning, 79, 106, reasoning controlled, 80; and self-control, 81–83, 89; and the "would-be," 114, 117, 127; becoming physical laws, 134, 136. *See also* Conduct; Self-control

Halley, E., 53

Hampshire, S., 75

Hanson, N., 49, 53 n.

Hartshorne, C., v, vi, 12, 139

Harvard, Harvard University, 2, 8, 11, 13, 15

Hegel, 20, 74, 100; Peirce's reaction against, 23, 68 f., 90, 103; Peirce compared to, 92, 96, 134; Peirce allies himself with approach, 108; influence of *Phenomenology of the Mind* on Peirce and Husserl, 128; "ignores the Outward Clash," 69, 133

Helmert, F. R., 3

Hempel, C. G., 58

History, 44, 125, 136

Hodgson, S. H., 17 n.

Hofstadter, R., 24 n.

Holmes, O. W., 6

Hooke, R., 53

Hope, 31, 35–38, 104

Hopkins, J. H., 10

Hume, D., 50, 75

Husserl, E., 21, 29, 128

Huxley, T. H., 24

Huygens, C., 53 n.

Hypothesis, 35, 36, 43–61, 64, 65, 74, 108, 124, 136. *See also* Abduction

Hypothetico-Deductive, 50–64

Ideal, 81, 82, 87, 88

Idealism, 7, 14, 33, 93, 95; important strain in Peirce, 98–106, 134 f., but not altogether, 117; Peirce's attack on, 101; and Pragmaticist, theory of

Index

reality, 114, 116; and real possibility, 115. *See also* British Idealism; Hegel

Indeterminacy, 76, 77, 126, 129, 133, 136. *See also* Chance; Tychism

Index, Indexical sign, 97, 98, 118, 133

Individuals, 23 f., 88, 118; social character of, 25, 82, 83, 109–10, 134; and welding, 38 f., 41; coherent theory of self lacking in Peirce, 89–90; reality is independent of a finite number of, 102. *See also* Secondness

Induction, 45, 130; Peirce's contribution to, 5, original account of, 124–25; needs no special justification, 35; continuous and cumulative, 40; and *"guiding principle* of inference," 81; validity, 104, 111; and methods of inquiry, 106–08. *See also* Deduction; Abduction

Inference, 46–51, 57, 64, 65, 79–81, 108 n., 124

Inquiry, 59, 91, 97, 98, 130, 137; collaborative nature of, 25; and 'Logic of Discovery,' 65; reality as the ultimate result of, 94–95, 134 f.; and the nature of knowledge, 102–19; science as perfect model of, 131. *See also* Community

Instinct, 28, 29, 81, 128, 135, 138

Intuition, 80, 83, 114; and scientific discovery, 72; Peirce rejects immediate, 108, 109

James, H., 24

James, W., 6, 16, 17 n., 19; mentioned, 8, 23, 31, 32, 67, 72, 100, 118; and pragmatism, 7; acknowledges and is influenced by Peirce, 7, 9; secures small fund for Peirce, 11; calls Peirce the most original thinker of their generation, 12; Peirce differentiates his views from those of, 123

Jastrow, J., 12

Jevons, W. S., 50

Johns Hopkins University, 8

Kant, I.: *Kritik der reinen Vernunft* a great influence on Peirce, 2, 18 n., 20, 21, 134; emphasis on formal logic an inspiration to Peirce, 6; sense of 'critical' important, 29; "distinction of regulative and constitutive principles is unsound," 35; Ideas of Pure Reason, 86; space and time as forms of intuition, 97 n.; method of metaphysical deduction, 126, 131

Kepler, J., 53 n.

Kernan, F., 12

Kierkegaard, S., 68, 69, 74

Klein–Gordon, 54 n.

Knowledge, 14, 67, 72, 107, 121, 125, 128, 130–32, 138; world united through love and, 17, 24; and faith, 21, 36–38; scientists and the exhaustion of, 25; and the nature of reasoning, 43, 83; structured in HD form, 52; "whatness" as primary object of, 71; and Thirdness, 72; and experience, 74; and the past, 78; and the community, 82; theory of, 85, causal theory rejected by Peirce, 94; Royce's conception of full and perfect, 97; of reality, 103, 104 n., 106–10, 114–19; methods of achieving, 137

Ladd-Franklin, C., 8, 12

Lagrange, J. L., 53

Lamarckian Theory. *See* Evolution

Laplace, P. S., 19, 53

Laws, 86, 107, 136; origin of, 7; conformity to is never perfect, 28; of nature, 29; classified as Thirds, 75, and Thirdness, 77, 100; not exhausted by past regularities, 78; and determinism, 125, 127–29; and chance, 127–29. *See also* Habit; Thirdness

Leibniz, G. M., 12

Index

Leverrier, U. J. J., 53

Lieb, I. C., 14, 18 n., 28, 30, 31, 37, 91 n.

Locke, J., 67, 74

Logic, 3, 39, 41, 67, 92, 97, 125, 127, 129, 135, 138; Peirce's career in, 3–13, 122; as 'critic of arguments,' 13, 29; German tendency toward, considered psychologistic, 20; and Pragmatic Maxim, 32; of vagueness, 33–36; and the natural sciences, 43–44, 46–49, 52–58, 65, 108–12, 136; as criterion for validity, 61, 63, for soundness, 80; and ethics and esthetics, 82–87, 139; of moral discourse, 86; social theory of, 103; no logical grounds needed for, 107 f.; and the community of inquirers, 123; found in all reasoning, 123–24; a method for classifying and evaluating, 126; metaphysics should be founded on, 131; an observational science, 132

Logic of Discovery, 42–50, 64, 65. *See also* Abduction

Long run, 24, 30, 36, 104–07, 110–13, 117, 118, 124. *See also* Induction

Love, 14, 17, 26, 30, 31, 40, 71, 111 n., 134. *See also* Agapism

Marx, Marxist, 68, 69, 127

Mathematics, 19, 50, 71; Peirce showed an early interest in, 1 f., 12; his contribution to, 4; his career in, 5; writing for *Century Dictionary*, 10, 13 n.; metaphysics the ape of, 40; religion welded to, 41; and the form of arguments, 50, 56 f., 58 n.; and logic, 123, 126; an observational science, 132

Maxwell, G., 46 n.

Mead, G. H., 136

Metaphysical Club, 6, 18 n.

Metaphysics, 7, 8, 10, 12, 31, 130, 132, 135, 139; Peirce's, 20, 111, is a species of absolute idealism, 21; is the ape of mathematics, 40; Peirce's bent toward, 93; "pragmatism is no doctrine of," 123; Kantian, 126, 131

Methodology, 85, 107, 126, 131

Milford, 10, 13

Mill, J. S., 17 n., 40, 44, 50, 114

Miller, P., 25 n.

Mills, E. H., 1

Mind, 115, 125; and body, 7, 66; and perception, 75; and Thirdness, 100 n., 132; the real is not external to, 101; not fixed or static, 105; and matter, 135, 136. *See also* Knowledge

Monad, monadic, 71, 72, 129. *See also* Firstness; Quality

Monism, 24, 136

Monist, 7, 8

Montesquieu, 19

Moore, E. C., 22 n., 67 n.

Moral, 81, 84, 86, 87, 91, 115, 135, 138. *See also* Ethics

Murphey, M. G., 13 n., 14 n., 18 n., 25 n., 30 n., 31, 91 n.

Napoleon, 12, 137

Nation, 10, 11

Nationalism, 15, 18

Natural classes, 126, 127

Negation, 90

Newton, I., 52

Nietzsche, F., 15

Nominalism, 6, 20 n., 21, 98 n., 127, 135

Normative, norms, 82, 83, 85, 86, 89, 133, 138, 139. *See also* Esthetics; Ethics; Logic

Number, 5, 8

Ontological, Ontology, 115, 123, 130

Opinion, 95, 99, 101–18, 134, 136, 137. *See also* Belief

Oppenheim, P., 58

Paine, H., 18 n.

Patterns of Discovery, 47–50

Index

93–104 passim; a matter of Thirdness, 96 f.; vs idealism, 97–104; pragmatic definition of, 114; and futurism, 118; and laws of nature, 127;
almost as obsession with Peirce, 135
Reality, 69; social theories of, 7; religious and scientific avenues toward,
25; and the categories, 70, 135; simple awareness is not knowledge of,
72; and lawlikeness, 76; Scotistic
view of, 79; Peirce's view, 92–119
passim; and universals, 127; close to
unreflecting common sense, 128; of
the indeterminate, 129; independent of ideas, 134; Peirce baffled by
the past, 136; of God, 139
Reason, 85, 87, 88
Regulative principle, 8, 35
Reichenbach, H., 43, 50
Religion, 11, 12, 24, 115, 119, 131;
Peirce brought up in Unitarian
household and joined Episcopal
Church, 14, 30; marriage of science
and, 14; and ethics, 24; and science,
24, 25–26, 36; and theology, 25; and
the Christian way, 30–34; based on
hate, 31, 33; dogmas and creeds are
overprecision, 33; and vagueness,
33–34; and logic, 39, 41
Renouvier, C. B., 19
Representation, 94, 98–106
Retroduction, 35, 40, 41, 47–64. *See
also* Abduction; Logic of Discovery
Robin, R., 22 n., 67 n.
Rorty, R., 70, 77 n.
Rousseau, J. J., 19
Royce, J., 7, 8, 12, 36, 93, 97, 100–02,
112, 116–18
Russell, B., 5, 67
Russell, F. C., 12

Sartre, J. P., 69, 74
Schiller, F. C. S., 17 n., 18 n., 44, 45, 123

Scholastics, Schoolmen, 6, 20, 88, 98
Schröder, E., 4, 41
Science, 24, 40, 108, 115, 125, 127, 135,
139; Peirce's career in, 2, 3; philosophy of, 2 f., 42–44, 122; Peirce's
contribution to methodology, 5; and
religion, 14, 24–28, 36; its methods,
22 n., 107, will reveal ultimate reality, 104; and theology, 24–25; and the
Logic of Discovery, 48–60, 63–65;
positivistic misstatement of, 86; an
activity of the community, 109–10;
its progress "is like the operation
of destiny," 112; limitations, 119;
inquirer in, 130; philosophy is a,
131; chemology and psychognosy,
132
Science, History of, 8, 12, 64, 111, 122
Secondness, 103, 132; criticism a variety of, 13; and categorial scheme, 69;
action is, 72, 77; other is, 73; Thirdness requires, but is not reduced to,
76; individuality, 90; force, power,
resistance, 94; reality belongs in, 96;
fact, 100; the "would-be" of behavior, 115; criticized, 132–34; antirational, beyond generalization, 137.
See also Dyadic Relation; Firstness;
Thirdness
Self, 73, 83, 89, 90, 91, 118
Self-control, 37, 77; Peirce lacking in
personal, 13, 91; Germans lacking in
intellectual, 18 n.; and evolution, 24;
its role in religion, 30, 31; in the
end, unnecessary, 34; conduct and,
67, 81–83; action and, 67; and experience, 69; and inference, 80;
needs norms, 83–84; and *summum
bonum*, 89; and Peirce's conception
of the self, 90
Self-criticism, 82, 83, 90, 91
Sellars, W., 85 n.
Semiotics, 5
Sense-data, 20, 105 n.

Index